CW00517084

# LIVE A BIG LIFE IN A QUIET WAY

LINDSEY HOOD

AND CO.

## Disclaimer

Lindsey Hood is a qualified life and executive coach but is not a licensed psychologist or medical professional, and her services do not replace the care of psychologists or other medical professionals.

All information outlined in this book is meant to help you identify the areas in your life, and in your thinking, that may currently be standing in your way of achieving the results you would like, and offer suggestions to help you make any changes you would like to. However, coaching is not professional mental health care or medical care. If you feel psychologically stressed or disturbed, to the point that it is interfering with your ability to function, please seek the help you need from a medical doctor and/or professional counsellor.

Lindsey's commitment to you in this book is that she is sharing her best professional efforts, skills, and care. However, she cannot guarantee your outcomes and her comments about the outcome are expressions of opinion only. You will be responsible for the results you achieve.

# CONTENTS

## DEDICATION

*I dedicate this book to my amazing, talented clients that inspire me every single day, to my wonderful parents for their continuous support and belief in me, to my brilliant brother for just being himself, and to my gorgeous husband for sharing his life and love with me.*

## LIVE A BIG LIFE IN A QUIET WAY

How different would things be if you realised, appreciated and fully embraced your own awesomeness?

The main challenge that the successful, talented women I work with face are they are amazing at what they do, they are considered an expert by their colleagues, they're respected and loved by their friends and family, their opinions are sought after, they're experienced, qualified, skilled, capable - but they don't feel it. Inside, they are feeling like a fraud, that it's by some luck, chance or odd twist of fate that they've achieved the success and position they have in their careers and life. I guess you're reading this because you are a successful, talented woman who is doubting her own awesomeness?

Somewhere along the way you have lost sight that it's your unique abilities, your individual strengths, and your personal attributes that have contributed to you being exactly where you should be in your career and life. I believe in living a life with no regrets. I believe you make the right decision at a point in time based on the information or feelings you have - if you didn't, you would have selected a different choice. This means wherever you are in your life is down to the decisions you have made, and these were always the correct decisions at the time they were made. Reconnecting with why you made the decisions in the first place can help you appreciate the journey you're on and what gave you the initial fire in your belly to go for something.

It's a bit unnerving at times to take full responsibility for your life; to take away the safety blanket of things happening to you, and accepting it's your own actions, choices and decisions that have led you to exactly where you are now - your career, qualifications, experiences, ideas and words swimming in your head. Accepting your place in the world, your thoughts, your emotions, everything is totally down to you, can be quite scary, confusing and also hugely liberating. If you got yourself to here (and here is an amazing place to be by the way!), you can also get yourself to somewhere else. You can be the master of your own destiny.

The risk is often you're so busy 'being' that you can't take that step back and decide what you want. You let your inner voice tell you you're no good, that you're a fraud and will shortly get found out, that you don't really know what you're talking about, that you're not the sort of person that can do

<insert your dream here>. It's exhausting to spend so much energy worrying about these things that, by virtue of you being where you are, can simply not be true. You let them hold you back, rather than focusing on building on your strengths or developing new skills to keep growing and developing. This is the state you choose to put yourself in.

You can say it isn't your fault. You can say you're conditioned to not have as much worth as a man. History has belittled women, put us as 'lesser' beings. How do you feel reading this?

I would argue that you can choose to feel differently about yourself. If you were describing your best friend, what words would you use? How would they describe you? Would you ever consider using these words for yourself? If not, why not? Maybe the part that hasn't been your fault is that you haven't known how to change, or not been fully aware of your thoughts and feelings. That's maybe why you're here today, reading this book, and realising that you want to spend your energy in defining and creating a life that you love on your terms, rather than staying in a state of worry, anxiety and self-doubt, and living a life that's so much smaller than you really want it to be.

You may already know, or have read about previously, some of the things that are discussed in this book, but please be open-minded to trying things. There is a difference between 'knowing' something and 'doing' something. You can know something intellectually, but until you experience it and do it yourself, you won't know if it works for you. I encourage you to be an explorer in your own self-awareness and self-development journey and embrace the exercises and ideas to be able to decide in an informed way, the ones that work for you.

You have the power to take charge and decide how you're going to feel and show up in your life from now on. I believe in you, and by the end of this book, you will re-believe in yourself.

With kind regards always.

Lindsey.

# CHAPTER 1 - LET ME INTRODUCE MYSELF...

I am an introvert who loves living a big life in a quiet way!

This one sentence is why I'm writing this book, but I want to share a secret with you, and that is I'm not that comfortable writing this book. My self-talk whilst deciding to do this, included the amazingly encouraging words of "Why would anyone want to read what you have to say?" "Everything you have to say has been said before," "You're not experienced enough, you're not clever enough, you're not good enough".

Does this reassuring and comforting self-talk resonate with you?

So, why do we do it to ourselves? Why do we say things we would never, ever say to anyone else? That's what we will be exploring in more detail throughout this book!

To totally prove I'm an introvert, I'm going to talk more

about me for a bit! My parents call me their butterfly, and my husband calls me his crazy monkey, as I get bored easily, and I am always looking for the next challenge. In my corporate career, challenging myself has meant constantly looking at ways to improve my skill set, and going for opportunities in exciting projects, or promotions, to continuously grow and improve. Taking challenging roles did expand and grow my abilities and experience - but every time I moved into a new position, which when I went for, I could see the possibilities and what I could bring to the role, there was always at least a 3-6 month learning curve, and with that came a crisis of confidence; I asked myself if I could actually do the new position - and just by asking the question, the self-doubt started to creep in.

With my confidence leaving the building it left me wondering when, not if, but when, my new manager would realise they had made an awful mistake and find me out to be a fraud - someone who wasn't capable of doing the job they'd employed me to do. I catastrophised the situation - my whole career would be in ruins, no-one would ever employ me again at this level, I would be a laughing stock - you get the picture?

I wanted to prove myself and prove that the person hiring me had made the right decision. I ended up working stupidly long hours, which could lead to many outcomes from feeling burnt-out because my work/life balance had disappeared, or resentful because I was looking at colleagues and wondering why they got to leave on time and have a life outside of work and I didn't, or, my absolute favourite, and possibly the pinnacle of my career, having an emotional meltdown in the office when that one unfortunate person said the one little thing that triggered me.

The doubt in myself could be crippling - and, at the time, working harder was the only strategy I had to get through it. I had sleepless nights worrying about the next day; I was constantly scared that today might be the day that I was proved to be the loser or failure I believed I was. It was over-whelming and exhausting, and I went through it every time I took on a new role or promotion. Yet, it didn't stop me from taking on new roles and promotions!

I would like to say this only happened in my career. Alas, this wouldn't be true, though. I collect experiences - I love trying new things. I have an ever-growing bucket list, and I want to achieve as much as possible before I die. These things range from learning some circus skills (just because you never know when you may need to run off and join the circus), running the London marathon, climbing Ben Nevis overnight, graduating with a Bachelor of Science Open Degree in my thirties, delivering public talks and workshops on imposter syndrome (even though this scares me, a lot, every single time!), renewing my wedding vows at the Little White Wedding Chapel in Las Vegas (whilst being serenaded by Elvis), dancing in a flash mob, being a volunteer at the London Olympic Games, jumping out of an aeroplane, abseiling down the Spinnaker Tower, making pots on a pottery wheel, busking for charity, performing in a burlesque show, and now writing this book.

I don't say any of this to brag. If you saw me before any and all of these experiences, you would've witnessed a woman filled with self-doubt; someone who wanted to give up because things seemed too difficult. I was outside of my comfort zone, and I battled with the internal conflict of wanting the experience, but not wanting to look like an idiot or to fail. For many of these now accomplishments, there were tears and tantrums. Yet once achieved, I spent little time celebrating before moving onto the next thing and starting this cycle all over again.

### *How did I break the cycle?*

I've always been interested in people: What makes us tick? Why are some people happier and more confident than others? Why do we sometimes have the motivation to follow our dreams and other times we prefer to stick with the status quo? I was attracted to coaching because it is forward-looking - it's accepting where you are, deciding where you want to be, and planning how to get there. I love a good strategy and felt a lot of what I did intuitively in life was aligned to coaching practices.

So, I made the life-changing career move to become a coach. As I embarked on my own journey of self-analysis and personal development, I realised that what I've just described, in both my professional and personal life, is a behavioural pattern, and when I researched this, it has a name - it is called the imposter syndrome. The training I undertook enhanced my own self-awareness and ability to 'experiment' with my behaviours to create effective strategies to improve my own performance - ultimately becoming the 'best version' of myself. By appreciating my natural abilities and strengthening these, I started to feel genuinely comfortable in my own skin. Being the real me takes less energy, gets great results, and people can easily get a sense of who I am and what I'm about.

Learning to accept myself for who I am - my perceived warts and all - has led to increased emotional freedom. Knowing what I bring to the party, and knowing where I want to develop have all strengthened my sense of self. So now, I can really show up. As me. No apologies. No trying to fit a mould. No worrying I will get 'found out'.

And I want to share this with you. I passionately believe that you have unlimited potential for change and with the right strategies, you can align your inner and outer worlds to live a full and harmonious life. I want to help you feel truly confident in your uniqueness, to see yourself as others do, to truly harness your natural skills to create and excel in a life and career you love, to wake up (after having a good night of restful sleep) knowing your worth and the value you are bringing to the table, to show up in all your wonderful glory!

So, maybe I should actually have started this chapter with:

Hey! I'm Lindsey - an optimistic and gentle life and executive coach for successful women who secretly struggle with imposter syndrome. I love, and live by, the saying by Mahatma Gandhi: "Live as if you were to die tomorrow. Learn as if you were to live forever". I'm constantly curious, I experience as much as I can, and I'm open to the opportunities life presents to be able to live the most amazing life possible, on my terms, as defined by me.

Are you ready to do the same? Are you ready to give yourself permission to be fully present in your life, to know yourself as well as you possibly can, to unapologetically stand tall in your awesomeness, to create a life you love, and to feel genuinely confident in the person you are? Yes? Then grab your journal and pen, so you can do all the exercises to make this happen for you, and read on!

(P.S. If you prefer to use a workbook for exercises rather than a journal, you can go to www.lindseyhood.net/workbook to download your free supplement.)

# CHAPTER 2 - IMPOSTER SYNDROME

Imposter syndrome is the feeling that you're a 'fraud', that you'll get 'found out', the belief that you're not good enough or deserving, and/or that you're out of your depth, regardless of the evidence, such as qualifications, training, experience, awards, and testimonials, to the contrary.

The term was first coined in 1978 by two psychologists, Dr. Pauline Clance and Dr. Suzanne Imes in their academic paper 'The Imposter Phenomenon in High Achieving Women: Dynamics and Therapeutic Intervention'[1]. Their paper details their five years of research with over 150 successful women where they found that high performing women, no matter their accomplishments, still remained convinced they didn't deserve their success or accolades and that they were, in fact, a fraud. These women dismissed their successes as luck or some kind of deception on their part in convincing someone they were better than they actually were.

I've taken the following from their abstract as over 40 years later; I find this still perfectly sums up the feelings I'm working through with my own amazing, talented clients:

---

"The term impostor phenomenon is used to designate an internal experience of intellectual phonies, which appears to be particularly prevalent and intense among a select sample of high achieving women.... Despite outstanding      academic      and      professional accomplishments, women who experience the impostor phenomenon persists in believing that they are really not bright and have fooled anyone who thinks otherwise. Numerous achievements, which one might expect to provide ample object evidence of superior intellectual functioning, do not appear to affect the impostor belief."[2]

---

In 1993 Clance co-authored an academic paper with Joe Langford, 'The Impostor Phenomenon'[3]. In this paper they suggest that society has lower expectations for what women can achieve, then, when we exceed these, we are more likely to put our success down to a cause that is external to us and our abilities.

However, in the same paper, they acknowledge that both men and women can equally suffer from imposter syndrome. Amy Cuddy, in her brilliant book, 'Presence'[4] reports other studies suggest as many as 70% of the population will struggle with imposter syndrome at some point in their lives, and she reports that Pauline Clance has later said she wishes they had called this the imposter experience because it's something that almost everyone experiences at some time, to some degree.

Although men do struggle with the feelings of being an imposter, it often feels more prevalent in women and the International Center for Research on Women and TRESemmé[5] back this up with their 2019 research stating that 88% of females experience imposter syndrome at some point in their lives.

I think these following factors highlight the possible gender differences:

1. Women are more likely to share their concerns and insecurities or be self-deprecating. This means because we are sharing our feelings, it seems that women are struggling more with this than men.
2. Feeling like an imposter can be exacerbated in individuals that identify as being under-represented in a particular area - for example, if you are the only woman on a board. When differences are called out, either positively or negatively, explicitly or not, it can

leave you susceptible to these feelings, questioning if you should be in a particular position because of your difference, or, worse still, questioning if you're only in this position because of the difference, and not because of your ability. [I just want to say if this example is ringing true for you, you absolutely deserve to be in the position you are in!]

3.  Women sometimes feel showing confidence will lead to some sort of rejection or double standard - for example, an assertive woman being described as bossy, which shouldn't happen but unfortunately still sometimes does. A way to avoid this is to not put any value on your unique attributes as you don't want to be seen in a negative way, but by doing this, you start to see yourself as lesser than you are as you're not standing in your unique awesomeness. This then lowers your confidence, and when you do stand in your awesomeness again, you feel like an imposter because you have got used to being 'lesser'.

### *Why do you feel like you're an imposter?*

There is much debate on why you feel like an imposter. Clance and Imes original research[6] suggests feelings of being an imposter may be perpetuated by the societal expectations of men and women - with women being seen as 'less intelligent/business-minded/strong' etc than men. I would like to think that 40 years on this is no longer the case, but the gender pay gap reports would suggest that this is still an issue [in 2020], and there are gender differences we still see in everyday life. An example is the need to name the female gender - "I saw a female doctor", "the first woman to...". These subconscious cues make being female something 'special' or different and that any achievements are even more amazing because you are female. Instead of feeling this though, you have more of a feeling of being an imposter because you identify as being a woman achieving something that you're being told, on some level, you shouldn't achieve in a 'man's world'.

Valerie Young in her insightful book 'The Secret Thoughts of Successful Women'[7] puts forward a couple of different suggestions. The first is you're heavily influenced by the messages you've received since childhood. Maybe you did very well academically and were called out on this by teachers, or maybe you have siblings and you were described as 'the clever one', and your brother or sister was 'the creative one' or 'the social one'. If you internalised this message, meaning it has become part of your identity, you would start to see yourself as academically inclined, aka 'the clever one'. When you stray outside your perceived parameters of 'being clever' or 'academic', for example maybe doing something creative like painting, or something athletic like cross-country running, or going out partying with friends, these activities are things you no longer easily identify as being part of 'who you are' - thus when you do them you feel like you're an imposter.

Issues may also arise if you're not as successful within your perceived parameters. For example, maybe you get a 'C' on a paper where you normally achieve 'A' grades. You may start to question your identity as you no longer feel you're 'the clever one' and maybe feel you have deceived people up to this point. In a world where the societal constructs mean you're always going to be compared to others, whether in an academic, work or general life scenario, and where bars are constantly being raised, labelling yourself, or allowing other people's labels of you to become part of who you believe you are, can be dangerous.

Your friend's opinions or, if you had the misfortune of being bullied, bully's comments, may also have shaped how you see yourself. Whether delivered as banter or with malice, words, as we will see throughout this book, can hold a lot of power. If we internalise the messages received, they will inform us of how we see ourselves - either positively or negatively, consciously or unconsciously. Maybe you identify as being the organised one, or the boring one, or the risk-averse one, or the risk-taking one, or the frivolous one, or the loud one, or the quiet one, or the privileged one, or the lucky one, or the unlucky one, or the fat one, or the skinny one. If these 'labels' become part of your identity then whenever you do things outside of these labels in any area of your life, you're susceptible to feeling like an imposter.

Another idea voiced by Valerie Young[8] is the subjectivity around how you measure success. Some topics are quite black and white - either you are right or wrong, such as mathematics or some sciences, but much of what you do in life is for subjective appraisal. Look at any film or book review, and you'll see a myriad of opinions - and that's all they are, an opinion on that piece of work on that particular day. This principle can also apply to school paper markings, work performance appraisals, as well as your own self-critiquing. So many other factors come into play that it's very difficult to get a fully objective view of your own strengths. You may struggle to ever fully appreciate your abilities, either dismissing accomplishments or compliments as someone having a wrong opinion on how good you are, or taking to heart a negative review as the ultimate truth rather than being just one person's opinion. (I will explore in more detail why it's easier for us to accept negative over positive feedback in chapter 6.)

In her book, 'The Imposter Phenomenon'[9], Pauline Clance describes how you might feel like an imposter if success comes very quickly or easily to you. In this situation, you might not feel that your success is real, especially if you grew up with the notion that you have to work hard to achieve; if you haven't worked hard, your internal logic would suggest to you that your success can't be real.

Conversely though, if things are difficult and you achieve them, you may also struggle with imposter feelings! Your

internal dialogue may be telling you that if you were naturally good at this, it would come easily, so the fact that you
had to put in additional effort means you're not naturally
good, so an imposter. The messages you have internalised
can mean you have lots of conflicting ways to argue your
way into feeling like an imposter!

However, the reason I'm most drawn to in terms of why you
struggle with feelings of being an imposter is this one: that
you think in a polarised way. What I mean by this is that on
some level you think "they are perfect; I am not", with the
'they' referring to everyone who isn't you. This way of
thinking is due to your own self-awareness. You can easily
recall the times you did something wrong, or an off-hand
comment that was said to you, or the struggles you've had in
learning a new task or understanding a particular concept -
and this is all internalised - you've made this part of the story
of 'who you are'. This means when you are doing something
outside of your comfort zone, you may see yourself as 'acting' rather than really feeling like you are 'being' a certain
way.

You then compare this to others. But the others are the
images you see - the airbrushed celebrities, the
Instagram/Facebook life of your friends, your manager that
seems so cool, calm and collected always. You don't think
about their struggles, that maybe they didn't find everything
easy, that this isn't how they are all of the time, that they
make mistakes and that maybe they are faking it! You take an

external view only - you see what they are showing the world, not what they are necessarily feeling. You don't see them as acting, but rather that is the way they are.

Both these views are your truth, but the comparison isn't fair: you're taking your external view of them and saying they are fully deserving of their status or situation - this is who they are, so by definition, they're not an imposter; and because you're acutely aware of everything you have been through in your life, you feel that you're not deserving because you don't think you compare to them, which means you must be an imposter.

However, you're not comparing apples with apples - well, not fairly anyway. You are comparing the cut open core of your apple, with their full, juicy, super shined up apple, that's ready for display.

To further illustrate this point, in 2018, I conducted some independent research on confidence[10], and one of the questions I asked participants was whose confidence did they most aspire to have. Michelle Obama topped that poll. Towards the end of 2018, Mrs. Obama is quoted as saying she still sometimes struggles with feelings of being an imposter[11].

Couple this with the statistics that almost nine out of ten women[12] either have, will, or currently are struggling with feelings of being an imposter, the 'them' you are comparing yourself to must, statistically, contain quite a few people that are thinking the way you are. People probably don't realise you're struggling with these feelings, because you're awesome at what you do, which is the same way you have no idea that they're also struggling with these feelings of self-doubt.

Remember, the image you see is not necessarily the same as how someone is feeling.

### *How can imposter syndrome affect your life?*

If you're feeling like an imposter, it can manifest and impact your life in many ways. Some of the common signs include:

## PERFECTIONISM

When you're holding yourself to an impossibly high standard, the risk is that every time you're less than perfect, it further increases your feelings that you are an imposter - because if you weren't you would be able to achieve these high standards, right?

Perfection is very subjective though. My idea of perfection isn't going to be the same as yours, and you tend to find you hold yourself to a much higher level than others do. I'm not saying you shouldn't try your best, and give your all, but what I am saying is you need to also put a perspective on this.

If, for example, you want to be the 'perfect' manager, what does that mean to you? What are the expectations of your staff and your own manager? Are they all aligned? Are they reasonable?

Have you considered there is no such thing as a 'perfect' manager because everyone has a different idea of what this is and that this will change over time and in different situations? What if I told you that maybe what you consider to be 'perfect' your team members don't care about - they just need you to show up and be a 'good enough' manager? And what if what you consider as 'not quite ready' may be someone else's idea of perfect?

When you try to be perfect, you tend to think in a black and white way - you're either perfect or you're totally incompetent! There are no shades of grey and the chances of being perfect, as outlined above, are slim, so you tend to spend more time in a negative and unresourceful state. This is why I rate productivity over perfectionism. By keep being productive, you're moving forward; you're learning and developing as you go - you can gain feedback and amend your approach/idea/thinking [if you feel the feedback is valid]. But you are getting your ideas out there; you're taking action, and you're showing up.

Remember, everyone is special, but no-one is perfect! Sometimes good is good enough and done is better than perfect.

## WORRYING

Worrying is your way of protecting yourself. It alerts you to the possible dangers ahead, and you then can stop yourself taking these actions. This has its place. Assessing risk is good, but you need to do it objectively and increase your self-awareness to know when you're 'catastrophising' a situation (when you take the worry to the absolute worst-case scenario and the probability of this happening to the highest), as this just causes anxiety and stops you making any progress.

### CASE STUDY

When clients are facing tough decisions and are worried, an exercise I play out with them is 'and then what?'. Below is a case study from a client who wasn't sure if she should apply for a new job.

---

**Client:** There is a great job opportunity, but I'm worried if I go for it, my manager will hate me.

**Me:** If that happens, then what?

**Client:** If I don't get the job, it will then be unbearable to keep working with my current manager.

**Me:** And then what?

**Client:** Well, I would hate going into work and would then need to look for another job but definitely couldn't find something that pays as well as this one.

---

At this point, I changed tact by asking: Is that true?

---

**Client:** Yes!

**Me:** There are no other jobs out there that pay as well or better than the job you are currently doing?

**Client:** Well, of course there are!

**Me:** Okay, so you feel you would need to look for another job, and there are jobs out there that do pay as well or better than the job you're currently doing; is that correct?

**Client:** Yes.

**Me:** And then what?

**Client:** Well, I suppose I would find another job, and that is kind of what I'm doing going for this job in the first place, and I would really love this one...

---

Sometimes playing out 'the worst-case scenario' takes the

fears from your head and when vocalised or written down, helps you put them into perspective.

My client decided to go for the promotion and was offered the job. In a subsequent session, she shared that she was now scared to take the position because she didn't feel good enough.

---

**Me:** If you accept the position, what's the worst that can happen?

**Client:** They will realise I'm a fraud and sack me.

**Me:** And then what?

**Client:** I will then lose my home because I can't pay for the mortgage.

**Me:** And then what?

**Client:** My marriage will break down as a result, and I will lose all my friends.

**Me:** And then what?

**Client:** I will be homeless and smelly.

---

Okay, this is quite a bleak worst-case scenario! My next question was: How likely is this to happen?

**Client:** Well, all of it, probably not that likely, but they will definitely realise I'm a fraud so it could happen!

**Me:** If it did happen, what are all the things you could do to turn things around? Let's brainstorm!

**Client:** Well, if I lost my job, we could move back home with my parents until I found another job. I could maybe look into apprenticeship schemes and begin my career again in a different field. I would definitely contact my network, and I think I'd be quite likely to get some job leads from there. Or maybe we could sell up and go travelling for a few months.

In reality, many of these ideas are not ideal for my client, but the purpose of the exercise is to show her that she is resourceful, and, she can find ways to overcome even the worst things happening.

Dr. Aziz Gazipura, a world-leading confidence expert states "fear does not necessarily equal danger"[13]. You often fear a particular outcome or situation, and you build this up in your mind to be awful and terrifying to face into: "I can't possibly give a presentation because I might forget what I need to say and freeze on stage"; "I don't want to tell my member of staff that their work is not optimal because they might not like me afterwards"; "I won't ask my manager for a pay rise because they may think I'm materialistic or may reject my request".

These thoughts cause you fear. They might be scary, but they are not necessarily dangerous. These things don't actually pose a threat to you, in some cases they may not even be true, but because you fear them, you avoid them.

The thing is though; you don't even know what the actual outcome will be! What if you give a great presentation and don't freeze? What if you give a presentation and freeze? What if your staff member thanks you for helping them improve? What if your staff member leaves? What if another staff member leaves because they're fed up with others on the team not working to an optimal level? What if your manager does think you're materialistic? What if your manager gives you a pay rise? What if your manager doesn't give you a pay rise?

There are many possible outcomes, yet you tend to focus on and worry about the ones that are the 'scariest' to you. Letting yourself play out your worst fears can do a few things:

1. It may end up making you laugh as you realise it isn't as bad as you thought and that you're catastrophising into scenarios that when said out loud, you know will never happen.
2. You realise that things will get bad, but you also play

out some scenarios to overcome the adversities, so you know you have the inner resilience and resourcefulness to cope.

3. You realise that things will get bad, and you're not willing to take that risk, so it isn't the right time for you to take that leap. This is a tricky one, as you could always go to the third option and never move forward. It's why working with a coach or mentor is useful as an objective third party. But there are scenarios that it really is in your best interests to not do something. Sometimes the cost is too great for the benefit you could receive, and then the best decision for you is to continue as you are. I often think you instinctively know what's right for you, as when you have made a decision from a place of rationality and logic, if you decide not to progress you feel lighter and there is no lingering sense of 'what if' or regret. Where this doesn't happen, I would encourage you to further explore your options to find a way forward that works for you.

## FEAR OF FAILURE

Struggling with imposter syndrome means you're already scared of being found out as a fraud, but you add to your ongoing anxiety and worry by wanting to be perfect, and when you're not, you live with the fear of failure. I love the saying "what would you do if you knew you couldn't fail?"

But what if there was no failure, just feedback? Yes, some mistakes are bigger than others, but the majority can be corrected or learnt from.

Clients I work with often worry about making an 'idiot' of themselves, but what is an 'idiot'? Like perfectionism, my definition is going to be different from yours. Maybe you're scared of failing and stepping outside your comfort zone; to do something where you might not achieve on your first attempt, makes you feel like 'an idiot'. Maybe you will 'fail', but someone else may look at you and think you're an idiot for not even trying! Everyone will have an opinion, and the only one that really matters is your own so think about, and analyse, what you believe and make it serve you.

And so what if you do make an idiot of yourself? Why do you think you shouldn't make an idiot of yourself? Why do you think everyone is so interested in you and what you're doing? Are you really that interested in everyone else? When someone does make an idiot of themselves, do you really care? Maybe the truth is that being human is about achieving someone's definition of being an idiot on a regular basis, and this is okay. Maybe a reframe of your thoughts is that you accept and embrace that being an idiot is part of being human. So, every day you know and expect to act like an idiot, at least once, as this cements your humanness and ability to move towards your goals.

If you let it, sometimes your fear of failure will hold you back to such a degree that your absolute genius can't come through. For example, you don't ask the pertinent question, you don't offer the amazing solution, you don't share your idea in the meeting, or you don't try the activity that will bring you joy or fulfilment. But what if by showing up fully, and sharing and trying and putting yourself out there, you solved the issue or created the required breakthrough or found a new fun hobby for yourself? You often forget that inaction, or 'playing it safe', also has a cost, and may be a greater 'failure' in the long term.

## OVERWORKING

This is one I completely relate to, where you put in more and more hours and risk burnout as you want to do a great job. But instead of working smarter, or accepting you are doing a great job already, you risk exhaustion. This then becomes a cycle because you know you're not doing your best work because you're now burnt-out, so you then try to put in more hours to prove yourself.

Everyone has the same amount of time in a day, but time is also one of the limited resources you have in the world. Once an hour, minute, second has passed, you're never getting that back. Think about how you want to spend your time and what you want to achieve, not just in one particular area but across every part of your life.

Saying yes to doing more in one area, means you're saying

no to using that time in a different way, in a different area of your life. Sometimes you'll want to prioritise a work project, but sometimes accepting you can only do a certain amount in a day, and spending time with your family, or going on a date night, or having drinks with your friends needs to become your priority.

## INNER CONFLICT

As an introvert, you may not want to be the centre of attention or may feel uncomfortable when you are praised, but it doesn't stop you wanting to be a success and achieve. You may feel it's undeserved, or you want to downplay when you do well, but you may feel resentful towards those that self-promote their ideas or accept publicity for their achievement. You may want more confidence in yourself, but find those that are constantly speaking up in meetings to be arrogant. You may feel like it's impossible to show up authentically as yourself as this is not what you feel society expects of you as you're a 'good girl' and have always been a particular way. You may feel like you're not ready to go for a work promotion, but feel annoyed that your co-worker is applying for it, even though he spends half his day asking for your advice.

These opposing ideas can create a huge amount of inner conflict and give you an uneasy feeling. To sort your internal turmoil, you may spend time trying to rationalise your feelings, but unfortunately, further side on the view that you're not good enough (because if you were, you would be doing the things you're in turmoil about) and others are more deserving (because they are doing the things you're in turmoil about). The uneasy feeling may subside for a bit because you have removed the inner conflict, but there is a price to your self-confidence.

The fact you have some inner conflict is highlighting to you that you want some sort of change. When you're feeling an emotion such as frustration, anger, fear or envy, let it be a guide for you. These are often great emotions for high-lighting what you really want!

You may never be the loudest voice in the room (if you are, that's awesome too, by the way), but over time, and with practice, it doesn't mean that you can't learn to accept a compliment, or enjoy giving your opinion in a meeting, or to show up in any given situation in whatever way feels right to you. By deepening your self-awareness and tuning into any inner conflict you might experience, you can choose to use this information as a way to find a different way of being, that is aligned to your values (more about values in chapter 4).


## UNDERMINING YOUR ACHIEVEMENTS

This may be self-talk, or what you say to others and often

has become so habitual that when you bring awareness to it, you may be shocked at the things you're saying.

Some examples may include saying or thinking your degree is from a lower-ranked university or is an 'easier' degree so anyone could have got it. Maybe when you're congratulated on getting a new job, you say or think that no-one else must have applied for the position, which is why you got it. Or maybe when complimented on your idea, you say it was nothing.

You may even use an achievement to hold yourself back in the future. For example, maybe you think you're being over-paid in your current position so you don't look for another job because even to get the same salary you feel you would need to be operating at a much higher level than you are currently.

You dismiss the fact that achievements are achievements. By undermining or belittling your achievements though you're further cementing those feelings that you are an imposter because you haven't internalised the achievement. By not owning your successes you're not putting any value into the effort, skill, experience, and abilities you must have to have achieved already and don't see this as part of who you are.

---

If you are identifying with any or all of the above, please

don't worry! Often your thinking and behaviours become habitual, and when you increase your self-awareness, you can then make a conscious choice if you want to change your thoughts and behaviours. We will explore this in more detail in the next chapter, but for now, it's for you to increase your awareness of how the imposter syndrome might be showing up and affecting your life.

### *You're not alone*

If you're struggling with feelings of being an imposter, you are in good company! In addition to Michelle Obama, there are so many reported cases of successful, amazing women, suffering from imposter syndrome.

In Grace Bonney's beautiful masterpiece, 'In the Company of Women'[14], I noted the following inspirational, artistic, creative women's comments:

---

"Q. Name a fear or professional challenge that keeps you up at night:

A. That I'm a fraud. That somehow, I have hoodwinked everyone into believing I'm better than I actually am."

— PREETI MISTRY, CHEF.

---

"When something good happens in my writing life - say I win a fellowship or an award - not too much time passes before little doubts begin feasting on my happiness, and my sense of self or accomplishment turns up dusty, moth-eaten. They made an error, the voices will say, or they gave such-and-such award to your work because you're Latina. Those kinds of doubts."

— CAROLINA EBEID, POET, EDITOR.

And a quick google search gives examples of many successful women who are feeling like a fraud[15] :

"You think, 'Why would anyone want to see me again in a movie?' And 'I don't know how to act anyway, so why am I doing this?'"

— MERYL STREEP, ACTRESS.

At the time of writing, Meryl has been nominated for the Academy Award an astonishing 21 times, and has won it three times, and has been nominated 31 times for the Golden Globe and won it eight times!

"I have written eleven books, but each time I think, 'Uh oh, they're going to find out now. I've run a game on everybody, and they're going to find me out'."

— Maya Angelou, Poet, Singer, Memoirist, and Civil Rights Activist.

"There are still days I wake up feeling like a fraud, not sure I should be where I am."

— Sheryl Sandberg, Social Media Executive, Author, Billionaire, Chief Operating Officer (COO) of Facebook, and Founder of Leanin.org.

"Sometimes I wake up in the morning before going off to a shoot, and I think 'I can't do this. I'm a fraud.'"

— Kate Winslet, Actress.

In 2012 Kate received a CBE (Commander of the Order of the British Empire) for her services to drama.

"I am always looking over my shoulder, wondering if I measure up."

— SONIA SOTOMAYOR, LAWYER AND JURIST WHO SERVES AS AN ASSOCIATE JUSTICE OF THE SUPREME COURT OF THE UNITED STATES.

"It's almost like the better I do, the more my feeling of inadequacy actually increases because I'm just going 'Any moment someone's going to find out I'm a total fraud, and that I don't deserve any of what I've achieved. I can't possibly live up to what everyone thinks I am and what everyone's expectations of me are'."

— EMMA WATSON, ACTRESS, MODEL, AND ACTIVIST.

"Even though I had sold 70 million albums, there I was feeling like 'I'm no good at this'."

— JENNIFER LOPEZ, SINGER, DANCER, PERFORMER, ACTRESS, FASHION DESIGNER, PRODUCER, AND BUSINESSWOMAN.

"I'm not even a good violinist... we all feel that way, especially about the things we are supposed to be the best at. We are so hard on ourselves... Sometimes I get really frustrated that I'm not as good as I think I should be. I feel like I'm an imposter in my own career sometimes - did I trick everybody?"

— LINDSEY STIRLING, VIOLINIST.

"When I won the Oscar, I thought it was a fluke. I thought everybody would find out, and they'd take it back."

— JODIE FOSTER, ACTRESS, DIRECTOR, AND PRODUCER.

At the time of writing, Jodie has received two Oscars, three British Academy Film Awards and two Golden Globe Awards.

---

"You will never climb Career Mountain and get to the top and shout, 'I made it!' You will rarely feel done or complete or even successful. Most people I know struggle with that complicated soup of feeling slighted on one hand and like a total fraud on the other."

— AMY POEHLER, ACTRESS, COMEDIAN, WRITER, PRODUCER, AND DIRECTOR.

---

"I've definitely been crippled by fear... At school, I was a contradiction. Outwardly, I was a confident, brave individual who went for it and was unafraid. But inside, I always had a niggle in my brain, moments of self-doubt, which made me question my abilities."

— ALESHA DIXON, SINGER, RAPPER, SONGWRITER, DANCER, PRESENTER, AUTHOR, AND MODEL.

---

Even royalty is not immune! Princess Beatrice at a Women in

Business event revealed "she suffers from the imposter syndrome every day and works to overcome it"[16].

However, although easier to find women declaring themselves a fraud, as stated earlier, there are just as many men that struggle with these feelings. Here are a few that aren't afraid to share their experiences with the world:

---

"I am not a writer. I've been fooling myself and other people."

— JOHN STEINBECK, WRITER AND NOBEL PRIZE WINNER IN LITERATURE.

---

---

"Very few people, whether you've been in that job before or not, get into the seat and believe today that they are now qualified to be the CEO. They're not going to tell you that, but it's true."

— HOWARD SCHULTZ, BUSINESSMAN, BILLIONAIRE, AND FORMER EXECUTIVE CHAIRMAN AND CHIEF EXECUTIVE OFFICER (CEO) OF STARBUCKS.

---

"No matter what we've done, there comes a point where you think, 'How did I get here? When are they going to discover that I am, in fact, a fraud and take everything away from me?'"

— TOM HANKS, ACTOR.

So, if external recognition of success isn't enough to convince you, regardless of the type of work you do, or life you lead, that you are amazing, then it suggests that feeling confident is an internal state. But how do you convince yourself you're genuinely intelligent, capable and deserving of the success you achieve?

### Good news, bad news

Feelings of being an imposter can be fluid - meaning they can ebb and flow over time - with some periods of your life where you feel very much like an imposter, and other times you'll have the inner confidence in your abilities. For me, this means the first 3-6 months in a new job role, or whenever I try a new activity, skill or experience I will feel like an imposter and these feelings will slowly disappear the more I do something.

You can also experience feeling like an imposter in one area of your life, for example, your career, but feel totally confident in another, for example, your relationships.

Later in this book, I will share strategies that can help you overcome feelings of being an imposter in a given situation, and empowering yourself to get into a more useful state where you can acknowledge and appreciate your awesomeness.

However, for full disclosure, I have some bad news for you: I don't think there is a cure for imposter syndrome. Unfortunately, if you're susceptible to these feelings, I think they're likely to keep arising every time you push yourself outside your comfort zone or try something new. The good news is I'll share with you how you can reframe your thinking, so this actually becomes a positive thing, as well as lots of other hints and tips so that when you have self-doubt or need a confidence-boost, you have many resources in your toolkit to do this. I know the strategies I share work, both from my own experience and that of the results and feedback from my clients, but they do require consistent action and implementation on your part.

## EXERCISE - TELL YOURSELF, "I LOVE YOU"

Self-love is powerful but isn't easy for many of us.

I was given this exercise by a coach who was working with me a few years ago, and it was surprisingly difficult for me to do! I had to stand and stare at myself in a mirror and say "I love you". To begin with, I couldn't hold my own eye contact. I then started laughing when saying it. What was going on?!

I could easily say [and mean] I love you to my wonderful husband, amazing parents, fantastic friends, but, when it came to myself, the words kind of got stuck in my throat. I was given a 30-day challenge, to keep saying "I love you" whenever I was in front of a mirror.

It did get easier. I did stop laughing. I did keep eye contact. I even smiled at myself. Learning to accept and love myself, as I am, really was a very special gift to give, and receive.

This is now what I encourage you to do as well. For the next 30 days, every time you see your reflection, tell yourself "I love you", for no other reason than you do. There isn't a condition attached to it. It isn't just when you feel you have done something well. It isn't when you feel you compare well to others. It isn't just when you feel you deserve it. It is every time you see yourself; you say "I love you".

## CHAPTER 3 - SELF-AWARENESS

My favourite definition of self-awareness is from Pathway to Happiness[1]:

"Self-awareness is having a clear perception of your personality, including strengths, weaknesses, thoughts, beliefs, motivation, and emotions."

Knowing yourself, including what gives you energy means you can utilise your own uniqueness to be able to implement simple strategies to show up in all situations in a way that's authentic to your true self. You'll find when you can do this, you'll achieve even greater results and feel confident in your actions, decisions, and communications.

You often think you're very self-aware, but without time and space to really consider everything you often have quite a superficial level of awareness. This isn't bad or a criticism but like with anything in life, if you don't take the time and effort to really work on something, then you're never going to become a master at it - our sense of self is no different.

Blind spots are called this because they are the things you can't see. In a car it's any part where you don't have visibility through the use of mirrors, or turning your head; in life, it may be accepting something about yourself without question or never exploring something to see if there might be a different action, reaction or behaviour that would produce a different result.

Identifying as an introvert, I never thought I could speak in public. Even the thought of it could make my pulse race and my palms become sweaty. I told myself I wasn't entertaining enough to speak up. I told myself no-one would listen to what I had to say because I wasn't experienced enough. I thought my accent was an issue, and my tone was monotonous. I told myself I was boring and I'd be wasting everyone's time if I said yes to speaking invitations.

I did try to overcome the fear. I went to a presentation course in my mid-twenties and ended up leaving before the end. The trainer asked me to speak louder, and I kept trying, but the feelings of humiliation became stronger and stronger, and the voice in my head tried to protect me by confirming I obviously wasn't good enough and so should run away. So I did.

I started to accept that I just wasn't the sort of person that gave talks. What I hadn't appreciated was the knock-on impacts on other areas of my life. You see, public speaking isn't just about addressing a roomful of people, it is anytime you share an idea in a meeting, or want to express an opinion with a group of people, or generally want your voice to be heard. This had become a blind spot, and it was only when a manager took me aside and asked why I wasn't contributing to our team meetings that things came to a head. I explained I wasn't going to speak for the sake of it. However, her counter-argument was I hadn't said anything in the last three meetings! Showing up wasn't enough, I had to contribute, I had to add value, otherwise what was the point of me being there? She coached me so I could say something right at the beginning of the meeting to help avoid the dread of speaking to build up as the meeting went on. She had faith that I deserved to be there, that I was good enough, but I needed to do my part to show everyone else this.

From this revelation years ago, I continue to push myself and no longer let this fear hold me back. In February 2019, I attended my first expo as an exhibitor and speaker. I took to the stage at the Olympia in London and delivered a 20-

minute talk about imposter syndrome and strategies to over-come it. It was terrifying, especially as my slides had gotten lost, so I did the talk with no notes or prompts. Fortunately, I had done a lot of preparation and practice beforehand, so I knew the structure and things I wanted to cover well. During the presentation, there were a couple of moments when my mind went blank, but I took a deep breath, looked across the 100 or so faces in the audience, and somehow, miraculously, the next words came to me. I know it wasn't the best public talk, I know my voice had a nervous quiver in places, I know my legs were shaking, and I know this is an area I want to continue to develop and improve on, but it was a huge step, and I'm so grateful for the experience and opportunity.

It's from taking this opportunity, that I got to work with the amazing Healing Business and delivered a unique mini-course for them, as well as delivered a workshop for Bare Retreats on imposter syndrome, and an exclusive webinar for Women Who Do on mindfulness. Each time I put myself out there, it is scary, but it does get a little easier. I think the next time will be hard again, as it has been a few months since I've spoken to a large audience in public. The years of negative self-talk and telling myself I'm no good at public speaking seem to become prevalent over the newly found confidence, but I know the strategies to help quieten the inner critic and quickly change my state to something more useful to me!

I had thought that acknowledging I wasn't very good at something was self-awareness, but it's more than that. I had jumped to a conclusion - that I was an introvert, and I was quiet and shy by nature. I let my fear of stepping outside my comfort zone mean I accepted this as part of who I was and I just would have hidden there, thinking I was self-aware, not realising the longer-term impacts this 'self-awareness' could have.

### *Mirror mirror on the wall*

Think about someone who annoys you. Now think about exactly what annoys you about them. Maybe they are always running late, maybe they are always 5 minutes early, maybe they seem overbearing, or maybe you wish they would make a decision. It doesn't matter, and you don't have to judge yourself for what you come up with - this quick activity is just to help you deepen your own self-awareness!

When you see something in someone else, you often experience annoyances because it's some sort of reflection on yourself. It generally is either:

- reflecting back something you can recognise in yourself and you don't like, or,
- it is showing you a behaviour you hope you'll never reflect back, or,

- it is showing you a behaviour you would like to have in some way but for whatever reason don't think you can display.

Imagine other people are a mirror and the things you notice most about other people are the things that are most important to you on some level. As an explorer in your own life, and without judgement, just sit with the things that annoy you and unpick the reasons why.

For example, if someone is always late and this really annoys you, are you also someone who is late and you are reflecting your annoyance about yourself onto them? Or, is it that you're never late, and it's a fear of yours to be late, so you're projecting this onto the other person? If you are late, does it annoy you? Is it a value your parents instilled into you that being late was disrespectful, shows disorganisation, or would mean you would miss out on opportunities? Or maybe you wish you could be more relaxed and occasionally not always be the first to an event?

This activity can also be used for things that you consider to be positive attributes that you see in others. To be able to identify an attribute, you must be able to identify into it. You cannot see kindness if you didn't know what kindness is, so by noticing it in someone else, you must have experienced this yourself.

So, when someone is annoying you or delighting you in the future, get curious and use it as a learning opportunity to understand yourself better. What is it about their behaviour that is annoying or delighting you? How is this a reflection on you? Is it a behaviour that you don't like in yourself? Or is it a behaviour that you fear? Or maybe it's a behaviour you would love to cultivate within yourself?

### Growth Vs fixed mindset

A fixed mindset is when you believe that you can either do something or you can't. It sees things as being permanent, for example, you either have confidence, or not, and this will never change. A fixed mindset lives in the now and doesn't allow for the possibility of change in the future. It's built into a lot of our societal constructs, such as the school grading system. Your feelings of worth become very much connected with someone else's measure of your success and achievements.

Conversely, a growth mindset believes skills and abilities can be developed and acknowledges that there is a learning curve and that any perceived failures are not permanent. You may not achieve what you want on the first attempt, but it doesn't mean if you keep trying, you won't achieve it in the longer-term.

Carol Dweck has done a lot of research into this area, and in her Ted Talk called 'The power of believing that you can improve'[2], she cites a study where a college would give students a grade of 'not yet' rather than a fail if they didn't meet the minimum passing grade requirements. This shift took individuals from seeing their grade as final, to seeing the future possibility if they continued to study and work hard.

You also need to be aware of your language around positive aspects. For example, if you say to yourself "I'm a kind person" - this is actually a fixed mindset. A more useful phrase may be something like "I like doing kind things and am always open to opportunities to be kind" - this acknowledges your achievement due to your own actions rather than thinking of this as a 'fact' or fixed behavioural trait about yourself. The risk of the first is that at any time you consider yourself not to be kind, you may then feel like an imposter when you next do a kind thing. You are a complex individual. There will be times that you might act 'out of character', or not aligned to your values, and you'll feel bad about this - but accepting you are human and sometimes make mistakes will stop you punishing yourself for a long time over your 'failing'.

If you're struggling with imposter syndrome, you're likely to be leaning more towards having a fixed mindset - for example, you think that you're not good enough and that you'll never be good enough. The risk with this though is you're not going to put yourself into situations where you might 'fail' because you see failure as something permanent and that it will further prove you're not good enough.

I use the word 'yet' a lot with my clients, and will also be using it with you in some later exercises! It's a really easy way to help move you from a fixed mindset to a growth mindset. If you catch yourself thinking or saying "I'm not good enough" - amend this to "I'm not good enough yet". I'm not good enough is final; I'm not good enough yet has the possibility of improvement and change.

Understanding your own limiting beliefs is part of developing your self-awareness. These may be things you're totally unaware of, and in chapter 6 we will be focusing on tuning into your inner voice to help you shine a spotlight on your own blind spots in this area.

At the moment though I would encourage you to start trying to foster a growth mindset by following this wisdom from Sháá Wasmund MBE in her book 'Do Less, Get More'[3]:

"Every day is an opportunity to learn something new and get better at something that is important to you."

Start accepting that things may take longer than you first thought they would. Start believing that who you are today doesn't have to be who you will be tomorrow if you don't want it to. Start realising that you have all the resources within you to create the life you want for yourself if you're willing to do the work.

### Strengths and weaknesses

In addition to trying to cultivate a growth mindset, I want you to also focus on your strengths. Developing a growth mindset will help you in all domains of your life, but is particularly useful when you're trying to improve in one particular area.

Societal constructs are pre-dispositioned to want to improve our 'weaknesses'. At school you're asked to focus on the lowest grade to try to improve it; at work, you have a performance review and are always given at least a couple of things you need to work to improve.

We are all unique, yet we seem to spend our lives striving to be like everyone else! When you are asked to focus on areas to improve, these are often things that the person giving the message is good at, so is relatable to them. It isn't to say you should dismiss constructive criticism, and there is always room for improvement, but I want to encourage you to balance your energies on developing your strengths rather than just working on an area that isn't as natural to you.

When you spend time improving your strengths (the things that you do easily, and/or you love doing) the chances are these will come so much more naturally to you and with minimal effort, you'll see large positive differences. Your strengths will enhance and make you stand out because you're so good at them, or the passion you have shines through. You'll feel happier and more fulfilled as you're doing more of the things you love and are aligned with who you are as a person or the values you have.

Compare this with using the same amount of effort for improving a perceived weakness. You may find you see minimal improvement, you might achieve mediocre results, or you may feel demotivated, or exhausted in the efforts, because it isn't something that's naturally aligned to who you are or what you love to do.

I do have a word of caution here: as I've said previously, I believe you can do anything you set your mind to, and I don't want you to confuse a 'weakness' with something you haven't learnt yet. As you identify and reach for goals you're likely to push outside of your comfort zone and try new things - this may be difficult as there is a learning curve, and it's at this point feelings of being an imposter often emerge, but until you try new things and practice for a bit, you won't know if they may actually be a strength of yours and something you love to do.

## EXERCISE - IDENTIFY, ACKNOWLEDGE, APPRECIATE AND DEVELOP YOUR STRENGTHS

Are you someone who dismisses the positives and focuses on what you feel you need to improve on? Do you downplay what you're good at, thinking that if you're good at it, everyone else must be as well? Maybe they are. But that doesn't diminish the fact that you're also good at it! It's the combination of things you're good at and your own style that makes you unique. Yes, you may have amazing organisational skills, as do other people, but you may also be great at data analysis and have a way of putting people at ease. Or maybe you're great at explaining complex ideas in a simple way, as some others may be, but it's the fact that you also can doodle diagrams that support your message that makes you different from other people.

So, in your journal, write down everything you can think of against the following questions:

- What are you good at?
- What do you love doing?
- What have others complimented you on?
- What are the positive things you have been told in your school reports, annual work reviews and/or testimonials from clients?

These examples can span your lifetime and can be added to

as you identify and develop new things you love doing and are good at.

You may remember things that have been long-forgotten. You may start to see trends emerging. You might be shocked at, and may even feel uncomfortable with, how many things you list. This is all good! Remember, this is for your eyes only and is to help you deepen your own self-awareness into the strengths you already have.

## CHAPTER 4 - VALUES AND MOTIVATION

*What are values?*

Everyone will have different values. The Collins English Dictionary[1] definition of values is "the moral principles and beliefs or accepted standards of a person or social group". Values are the things that you feel or believe are really important to you, and I think it is deeply linked to increasing your self-awareness. Some of your values will be due to the messages you received as you were growing up, whilst some will be down to your own experiences of the world. They will often inform your behaviours and actions. Without knowing what your values are though, you're likely to not have control over these. This means when you do something that is out of alignment with your values you may feel 'icky' - that feeling in your gut that something isn't right or you're at odds, but you can't really explain where the feeling has come from.

Within my own career, I remember taking a job that was a brilliant position for my skill set, but the company didn't align with my values. I took the role because a fixed-term contract had come to an end, and I felt I didn't have many other options available to me at the time. Even at the final interview, my gut was telling me something was wrong, but I ignored it; within the first couple of days of starting, I knew I wanted to leave.

The company itself wasn't necessarily doing anything wrong, but it wasn't aligned with my values, so I never felt comfortable there. Before this experience though, I hadn't thought much about my own values or appreciated how important it is to ensure my values are being supported in all areas of my life.

I think this question from Valerie Young[2] is the best way to help you identify your own values:

---

"What am I not willing to sacrifice in order to have money, status, and power or to otherwise succeed?"

---

Maybe for you, it is confidence, decisiveness or efficiency; maybe it's openness, friendship, and building relationships;

maybe it's cooperation, sincerity or dependability; or what about expertise, competency and objective reasoning?

Here are my top values:

- Security
- Compassion
- Equality / fairness
- Integrity / authenticity
- Positivity / optimism

I think it's important to know your values because you can then align your life around these. Understanding what your values are can take some work though - I know it did for me! I worked with a business coach when setting up my coaching practice and was surprised at how important [financial] security was to me. I think previously in my working life, having an income was never something I really thought about, so moving to a self-employed status, and the uncertainty around this, created a lot of resistance in me. If I hadn't worked through this though and accepted that security was important to me, I may have pushed ahead to go full-time into coaching (which may have led to a lot of anxiety for me) or the opposite, of never trying at all. Instead, by acknowledging this value, it meant I could then start being more resourceful and finding solutions that were aligned with my values. I now have a portfolio career: I work part-time as a Talent and Development Manager for an amazing tech company, and I work part-time in my coaching practice.

I had always thought of myself as an 'all or nothing' individual, so until doing this personal development work, a portfolio career hadn't even entered into the equation. But deepening my self-awareness, and uncovering something previously unknown about myself meant I could make more informed decisions and create a life that felt secure and authentic to who I am. Living this way means I don't feel like an imposter because I'm embracing what's important to me and creating a life around these values.

## *Motivation*

The Collins English dictionary[3] says "your motivation for doing something is what causes you to want to do it... [It is] the process that arouses, sustains and regulates human and animal behaviour". This means your motivations are what are driving your goals and need to achieve these, and are generally aligned to your values.

There are many theories on motivation. Fundamentally though, all motivations are internal, and they are generally governed by your emotions or values, rather than the logical aspects of decision making. In other words, motivations are often led by our heart rather than our head!

Bevis Moynan[4] specialises in motivational mapping and

suggests you're likely to be motivated by relationships, achievements or growth, but within each of these categories, there is a wide variety of factors and values. For example, within achievements your motivators may be to master a skill, to lead a team or to earn more money; or within growth, you may be motivated by doing things that you feel make a difference, or give you freedom, or allow you to be creative; in relationships, your motivators could be security, friendship or respect. So even within a broad motivational topic, you can see how the specific values and things that are important to you will lead you to need to pursue different paths.

So finding your 'why' is important to help with motivation. Making your reason for achieving so important to you, knowing what you'll feel, see, hear when you succeed and knowing why you really want this is a great first step to supporting your motivation. For example, I wanted to participate in a mini-triathlon. I decided that I wanted to be fit enough to swim 500m in open seawater, cycle 15km and then run 5km - I wanted to know I could push myself and train and achieve this goal. I could visualise myself running out of the sea, changing out of my wetsuit and grabbing my bike, the crowd cheering as I cycled along the roads; I could see myself crossing the finish line, sprinting that last 100 metres; I could feel how amazing it would be to push my body further than I ever had before. I know this motivation may be different from other people's that are taking part in triathlons, or other sporting events, and it doesn't matter. What matters is that I had a strong reason to do this that mattered to me. This meant when the training got tough, and I didn't want to get up at 5 am to go for a training run before work, or I wanted to go drinking at the weekend but couldn't because I knew I wouldn't be able to then do the hour swimming practice on the Sunday with a hangover, it helped me stay focused on the bigger, longer-term motivation, rather than my short-term need.

What do you care about? What is important to you? What do you want to achieve in your life and why? Understanding this, I believe, is an important step to sorting your motivation.

### *Procrastination*

Increasing your self-awareness is a continuous process because you're always growing and developing. When you think you want something and you put off achieving it though, there might be some underlying reasons to investigate.

Procrastination isn't about being lazy; it is about how you're feeling about the situation you're facing into. Procrastination may even be your stress reliever! When you procrastinate, it's often because part of you is resisting the change you think you want because there is an unresolved conflict or an unconscious benefit you are receiving from your current state. No matter how much you think it's undesirable, there will be some benefits, otherwise you would have already made the change you think you want to make.

Let me show you what I mean:

Do you want to overcome imposter syndrome and increase your confidence? Of course - that's why you're reading this book! By achieving this, you would know who you are, what your values are and live your life aligned to these; you wouldn't doubt yourself and could create a life you love on your terms without fear that others would disapprove; you would take opportunities knowing you have the inner resources and resilience to be successful; having more confidence in yourself would mean you feel comfortable giving your opinions, participating in conversations and showing up fully in your life.

But staying as you are means you're within your comfort zone; you've always been plagued with self-doubt and aren't sure what life would be like to not have this; you can feel resentful and hard-done-by; you don't have to risk being seen and heard; you can keep playing it small; you don't have to take responsibility for doing the mindset work to change; you're safe and protected.

Do you hate your job? Getting a different job means you could experience more job satisfaction; you could make more money; you may take a new career direction; you're happy on a Sunday because going to work on a Monday excites you!

But staying as you are means you have enough money to pay your bills; you don't have to spend time and effort searching for a new job; you avoid any disappointment of not getting an interview; you get sympathy when you complain about your terrible boss.

Do you want to be in a loving relationship? Maybe you're fed up with being single and want to share the adventures of your life journey; maybe you want some company in the evenings and someone to go on holiday with.

But staying as you are means you have your freedom to do what you want, when you want to, with no compromise; you don't have to be vulnerable and open your heart to strangers and risk getting hurt; you get to choose the TV channel, what to eat and you get the whole bed to yourself every night.

Do you want to be healthier? Being fitter may mean you would feel more comfortable in your clothes, your blood pressure decreases, and your skin looks clearer; you may have more energy as you eat healthy, high energy food and drink plenty of water; you may feel calmer and happier; you could run for the bus without looking like a sweaty tomato.

But staying as you are means you don't have to get up early to exercise; you can eat a packet of biscuits whilst watching

TV in the evening; you can order a takeaway when you don't want to cook a couple of times a week; you don't have to risk failure of not achieving a fitness goal; you can gossip to colleagues during your cigarette break; you have an existing wardrobe of clothes that fit you fine, and you don't want to be wasteful.

None of the above is bad. It's just trying to illustrate that the reason you sometimes can't make the change you think you want to make is because of the fact your current situation does have benefits, and until the benefits of the change are significantly more than the benefits of your current situation, you're likely to remain unmotivated to change. Becoming aware of how your current situation is serving you means you regain power by being able to control your motivations and align with your core values.

Remember, if you're not making the changes you think you want to, you're protecting yourself in some way. Change is scary, and although you don't want to stay in your current situation, your current situation is what you know.

Fear is your mind's way of trying to protect you. When you perceive danger, a chain reaction begins in your body where your heart rate quickens. Your breathing becomes more rapid. Blood is pumped to your muscles as you prepare to either fight the perceived danger or flee from it. This is brilliant when there is actually a danger that is going to cause you some sort of harm, such as an animal attack.

However, you often have this reaction when you're not actually in physical danger, such as before giving a speech or taking an exam or doing something new. Nerves can be good, but debilitating fear, when you avoid doing something because you fear it, is not.

As you go to move into the unknown and stretch outside your comfort zone, stressors are released in your brain and to keep you 'safe' your brain comes up with lots of other things you could do instead to distract you from the harmful activity. You use displacement activities - other things that need doing - to distract you and keep you busy, so you don't face the stress of the more challenging work that you need to do to achieve your longer-term goal or dream. However, this is short-term because you still need to do the work, and now you may also have feelings of guilt, anxiety or higher stress because you have less time to get the work done in!

This is why you need to really understand your values and motivations, your why, because otherwise, you're relying solely on willpower and willpower alone is very difficult to sustain. Ultimately, you're trying to keep control (power) over yourself (will). It's so much easier to revert back to old ingrained habits than to continue on a new path. The immediate pleasure you'll get from doing something that goes against your longer-term plan (for example, eating a cake) may be greater than the distant pain you'll feel by not accomplishing your goal (for example, losing a stone and being healthier by summer).

In 'The Power of Leverage'[5], Tony Robbins says you're motivated either towards pleasure or away from pain. Moving away from pain tends to be short-term (as you're trying to reduce the pain the quickest way possible and have some form of immediate gratification) compared to moving towards pleasure which is for the longer-term (delayed gratification). This is why, until your current situation is so painful to you, you may find it difficult to make the changes you think you want to make; the pleasure you're moving towards (your end goal) feels too far away, and the pain isn't enough for you to want to move away from it.

To get real traction with your changes, you can identify and concentrate on the pain with your existing situation, and find ways to receive immediate pleasure in taking action. You need to make doing nothing more painful to you than taking the actions to achieve your pleasurable outcome.

For example, if you want to be more confident, focus on what lacking confidence is currently costing you. Focus on the pain you feel at being unseen and unheard at the moment and all the great ideas you haven't been able to share. Remember those feelings of self-doubt when you haven't been able to speak up, and you know you missed an opportunity due to your lack of confidence to go for something. Really feel the dissatisfaction of playing small and being overlooked and that these feelings could continue for the whole of your life if you don't make a change.

Now visualise how you'll look, sound, feel and act with more confidence, and how others react to, and interact with you. Imagine the opportunities that will come your way when you're confident, the projects you'll be invited to work on, the meetings you'll contribute to, the promotions you'll be able to go for, the experiences you'll take part in, the relationships you'll have. Think about how amazing it will feel to achieve these things, to succeed in all these new and exciting ways. Hear the compliments that people will have about your ideas. Sit taller, hold your chin higher, breathe deeply. Decide you will discuss a new idea you have with your manager later today or book on a course you want to study or research a holiday destination you're interested in travelling to.

In the above example, you have intensified the pain so much that you need to make a change to get away from this situation - it is now truly undesirable to you. You've also made the pleasurable alternative (your goal) real, tangible and have identified an action you can take today to start moving you towards this (immediate gratification). You have controlled your thinking, so your current situation is no longer serving you at all, which creates immense motivation to achieve your desired outcome.

## EXERCISE - IS YOUR LIFE ALIGNED TO YOUR VALUES?

1. Spend some time thinking about what your values are and make a note of these in your journal. [If you need some help with this, refer back to the beginning of this chapter.]

2. In your journal, over the next week, keep a note of all the activities and things you do. This might look something like this:

---

Monday - dropped dog at doggie day care; 2-hour train commute to work; working on a project; lunch with a colleague; 1-hour team meeting; 30-minute client call; catch up on emails on the 2-hour commute home; picked up the dog; dance class; dinner in front of the TV with partner

Tuesday - 30-minute home yoga session; working from home today; checked emails received overnight; progressed with risks and issues log on project; took dog for a walk during lunch hour; continued with risks and issues log; had to work urgently on resolution after notified of a mistake that has been made on the project; cooked dinner etc

---

3. After you have collected this data, review the list and put a

small tick against each activity that you feel is aligned to your values, and a small cross against things you feel are not aligned to your values.

**Tip: Don't spend too long on this step - go with your gut instinct.**

When I ask clients to do this exercise, it can be quite enlightening as they may realise they are spending a large portion of their life doing activities that are against their values which could be a contributing factor to why they are struggling with imposter syndrome. For example, they realise for the first time that a large part of their working life is about conflict resolution within their department, and their values include self-reliance, simplicity, and having inner harmony.

Knowledge is power, so understanding where you're spending your time currently can give you the information to decide if you want to make changes. In the example above, the individual may decide that a career change is required, but they could also decide that they have never really understood how to handle conflict so training in this area may equip them with the skills to be able to do this more effectively and possibly in ways that do feel more aligned to their values.

Sometimes it's just a small change or a mindset shift that can make a big difference. For example, if you value continuous learning, but you feel that you've been doing the same job for the past five years, you can decide to start seeing learning opportunities in interactions you're having with others, or you can decide to use your lunch breaks to learn a new skill. Or maybe you value your friendships but realise that you're working really long hours, so you can decide to carve out an evening a month to meet with friends for a meal.

It's about finding ways to create time for more activities that support your values as this will help you feel more aligned and on purpose. Self-doubt will diminish because you're aligning your inner world (your values) with your outer world (your actions). It will also mean you'll be more motivated to stick to any changes you want to make and achieve what you want to do!

## CHAPTER 5 - CONFIDENCE

Confidence is often cited as a key attribute required for success. However, defining confidence can be difficult, and I think this is because it means different things to different people, based on your experiences, upbringing, and beliefs. Confidence comes from a Latin word meaning 'to trust'. The Collins English Dictionary[1] refers to confidence as a feeling - that you feel you have certainty or trust in someone or something.

If confidence is 'to trust' then self-confidence literally means to have trust in yourself. To me, being able to trust in your abilities, your experiences, your skills, your ideas, your qualities, your worth - that is self-confidence.

Confidence is often linked to your ability to do a particular skill or achieve a specific outcome, whereas self-esteem is more connected with your self-worth and the value you place on yourself. In this way, I feel increasing your self-esteem will lead to longer-term confidence in yourself. Some use the terms interchangeably, and they are definitely connected. You will find that if you have high self-esteem, you're likely to be confident, and equally, if you have low self-esteem, you're likely to not be confident about your own abilities.

In September 2018, I conducted my own independent research into confidence[2]. Self-worth, self-belief, and self-assurance were the keywords used to describe what confidence meant to respondents. 63% of participants thought lacking confidence had a negative impact on their career, but only 12.5% said they felt very confident already within their careers, with a massive 81.4% stating they wanted to feel very confident. Out of the respondents who identified as being female, only 9% felt very confident, compared to 29% of respondents who identified as being male.

There are many benefits perceived in having more confidence, including:

- being happier
- stopping the fear of judgement from others
- fully showing up as your true, authentic self
- valuing your own opinions and beliefs
- doing things that currently scare you
- communicating better with colleagues, friends, and family

- taking more action
- making better decisions

From this list, it's clear why we want higher self-confidence!

As someone who lacked confidence, for years I thought it was because I was an introvert, and unless I could become an extrovert, and be comfortable talking in front of people and be seen as very charismatic, dynamic and assertive, I could never be seen as being confident. I also thought of confidence as a steady-state - where if I ever achieved it I would always have it - so anytime I felt confident, the next time I didn't, it further cemented my feelings that I would never be a truly confident person.

These thoughts became self-limiting beliefs and held me back from appreciating what abilities I did have by focusing on what I thought I lacked. Learning more about confidence and changing my own perceptions and understanding helped me greatly. I've learnt that confidence is about accepting who you are and believing in yourself. It's about being true to who you are and your values and living with integrity and authenticity. It's about appreciating and being proud of your accomplishments, even if you choose not to tell everyone about them. It's about knowing and trusting in your capabilities and achievements - this then builds the belief and love in yourself. Confidence isn't about being fearless, it is about being courageous – and in the words of the brilliant psychologist Susan Jeffers[3] – it's about feeling the fear and doing it anyway!

### Why does confidence come and go?

I think there are a few reasons confidence can ebb and flow over time.

## EMOTIONAL STATE

Confidence is a feeling, and like any other feeling, there will be times it's stronger, and other times it's less dominant, the same way you're not happy or sad or angry or passionate all of the time. When you do something you feel proud of, or receive a compliment that resonates with you, or achieve something you have been working towards, your confidence is likely to be higher.

I believe true confidence has to come from within you. It is trusting in yourself and your abilities. The more you can do this, the more that underlying feeling will remain constant in your life, even if it's at a lower frequency than the 'highs' mentioned above. If you can take the 'highs' and internalise these, they can become part of who you are.

## GENETICS

In 'The Confidence Code'[4], Katty Kay and Claire Shipman's research indicates that scientists believe between 25% and 50% of your ability to feel more or less confident is dictated by your genetic makeup. However, this also means that life choices and events matter as much, or more, than your natural predisposition.

Neuroplasticity is the premise that your brain can continue to change throughout your life. It has the ability to create and develop new neural pathways for different responses to stimuli which gives you more options to the situations you find yourself in. This means you can choose to take action and consciously think differently about things, and over time you will rewire your brain for this to become your new norm.

## *CASE STUDY*

An issue I worked through with my client was that she wanted to be more social at work, but felt too shy and that she had been there too long to now make changes to how she interacted with colleagues. We agreed on an experiment, where every time she went and got a coffee, she would say something, even if it was just "hi" to at least one person she saw in the office. This felt doable because it wasn't a 'wholesale change' to her personality or behaviour. It was a small action, that was linked to another specific action.

She was amazed by how easily conversations were struck up from this simple activity. Sometimes people just said hi back, but often people would ask how she was, or she would offer to get them a coffee as well, and conversations started to flow from there. Her brain was being rewired from thinking she was a shy individual, to that she could easily have conversations with co-workers.

If you're predispositioned to be less confident, it means you may have to work a bit harder than someone who already naturally feels more confident, but you can train yourself - and the strategies in this book will help you find ways to do this that work for you.

## MOVING OUTSIDE YOUR COMFORT ZONE

You sometimes lose confidence in yourself when you're trying to do something new. Confidence builds when you do things and gain competence, so it isn't surprising that you don't feel confident when facing the unknown.

If you think of confidence as a feeling, you can relate it back to other times you have felt confident. In this way, confidence can be seen as a transferable skill. You can cultivate the belief in yourself that you can figure out how to do whatever it is you're facing because you have figured out many other things previously. Confidence then moves from focusing on knowing how to do the [new and unknown] task, to you as an individual, and your ability and resourcefulness to overcome challenges.

Executive coach and motivational speaker, Caroline Miller[5] explains that mastering a skill is about the "process and progress". As of June 2019, it's reported that over 1.2 million pieces of new data are being produced by social media users every day[6] - you're never going to be able to consume every bit of knowledge or information that is now available or will become available. It's about learning what you need to know at any given point in time, doing the work, improving your competencies, learning to accept and overcome the challenges, and that you might not be the best, or may always struggle with a particular aspect, but you never stop trying. This is because it's the act of trying, and doing, and learning as you go, that is actually how you master a skill. Caroline goes on to explain that you get the added benefit that your confidence also grows as you progress and go through the learning process. By not forcing yourself to be the best, by accepting where you're at, and keeping going and trying, you're building your inner resilience and your inner confidence.

Accept that there is a learning process when you're trying something new and try to reframe your thinking to something like "I don't feel confident yet, and that's okay because I'm learning and growing" or "I'm feeling like an imposter, and this is a good thing because it means I'm developing new skills and experiences". Try these reframes and see if they're more useful to you when you're next moving outside of your comfort zone.

## CONDITIONAL v NON-CONDITIONAL CONFIDENCE

Confidence is often connected to external factors - for example, you may feel confident when you get a job promotion, or you have a new hairstyle. This is known as conditional confidence because you feel confident because of a particular reason (a condition). If these external factors change though (for example, you get demoted or lose your job; or you have a bad hair day), and if you haven't internalised the feeling of confidence, then your confidence can go when the external factor changes.

Also, when confidence is linked to external factors, such as your manager's approval, or your friends loving you organising everything in the group, there is the additional risk that you won't take certain actions for fear that this confidence will take a dip if you do something they don't like. For example, maybe you need to let your manager know of a problem that will have long term impacts, but you know they won't like to be made aware of this, or maybe you don't have the time or energy to organise the tickets for the festival this year. In both these examples, if your sense of self-worth and confidence is linked to how others perceive you, you may not take the actions that are right for you and end up doing what you think others want or expect of you.

On the other hand, non-conditional confidence is accepting yourself and having self-worth regardless of any external factors - you're separating your feelings of self-worth from your capabilities. If you don't receive a compliment, you still know you have value; if you have a bad hair day, you know that you offer more to the world than just great hair. I think non-conditional confidence is true self-confidence because you're totally trusting in yourself in any given situation. It's still nice to get a compliment from your manager or friend, but this is then the 'cherry on the cake' and not the whole cake as you know you have taken the right actions, and done the right thing for you.

When you struggle with imposter syndrome, you often will experience conditional confidence - you only think you're good when you do X, Y, Z [perfectly]. You may have linked your confidence to your ability to do a particular skill. This is generally on a scale of competence where you need to feel like you achieve a minimum standard and often, you're comparing yourself to others, so feel you need to achieve a greater level than someone else. Alternatively, you may feel confident depending on your comfort levels in a particular situation, so anytime you venture outside your comfort zone, your confidence disappears.

You don't always value yourself, your journey, and the effort it takes to sometimes just show up and try. You've said to yourself on some level that you'll only feel confident and worthy when you have achieved X rather than appreciating yourself and having self-worth now whilst still striving and working towards a goal.

If you understand yourself and your values, you can achieve non-conditional confidence. It's independent of your skills and circumstances. You're unaffected by external factors because you have disassociated your feelings of confidence with specific situations and value yourself as an individual. I know this sounds vague and quite spiritual, but it is an important concept to try to get your head around. A practical way of doing this is instead of focusing on the 'how' of a situation - how you will do a particular job, or perform a particular skill, focus on what you're trying to achieve - your purpose or why.

### CASE STUDY

Having worked with my client for several sessions and seeing progress towards her business goals, she came into the fifth session looking deflated. She had successfully planned out a workshop format and then when in the workshop, felt the plan went out the window due to the differing needs of those in the room. When explored in more detail, she admitted she had received great feedback. When I asked what would've happened if she stuck to the plan, it was noted that it would've been too technical for some attendees and not technical enough for others - so adapting on the day to the needs of those in the room is what gave them value. I think this comes down to expectations over reality. We talked about how it's good to have an idea of how something will go, visualise this, but it's the outcome that is important; for her, the outcome is to give maximum value to her clients. The actual execution of the workshop looked different to her expectations - but if it had gone to plan, the outcome she wanted wouldn't have been achieved!

After working through and reconciling this, she decided she would amend the workshop description, so it was more aligned to her style of having the knowledge and giving what is required to the individuals on the day. This then aligned her and her attendees' expectations.

During the last few weeks of working together, my client learnt to 'care less' about the 'how' of her business and to focus on her real objectives - earning more money and her work/life balance. The work is different from what she had thought, but she is enjoying it, and there is a 'buzz' about what she is doing. She has also reported that she has had a lot more engagement and enquiries. She is more confident to try things because she is trusting in herself and is not attached to the outcome - things may work, but if they don't, that's okay, she will evaluate, decide if she wants to try again, or move on.

## *Do you fear being confident?*

You sometimes might have a resistance to becoming more confident because you fear you'll become complacent, or arrogant, or stop being who you believe you are as it isn't aligned to your values. As an introvert, you may think being confident isn't part of your personality because you're quiet by nature, or prefer your own company, and don't want to put yourself 'out there'. Maybe you're worried that people won't like you or you think that you can either be nice, or be confident, but not both.

However, I don't think it needs to be this way. You can feel certain about your abilities, your worth, your qualities - this is confidence - but you can also continue to be your true self and live with integrity and authenticity. You don't have to tell everyone about your accomplishments if you don't want to, but whether you tell people or not, your achievements are still there, and so you can have the [inner] belief in yourself and what you're capable of.

The opposite of confidence is timidity, pessimism, being afraid, shyness, being uncertain or unsure. Is that really how you want to be viewed by others? Reframing how you see confidence and understanding there is nothing wrong with being positive, courageous, certain, self-reliant and self-assured, can help you break the self-talk that stops you feeling confident and fully showing up. It's okay to hold your head high and know your value and what you can achieve.

You can be confident and still be a nice person. You can be confident and still be empathetic, fun, goofy, serious, caring, loud, introverted, <insert your most treasured characteristic here>. Being confident is not mutually exclusive to all other traits; it is totally compatible.

### The skill of confidence

At school, college and university you're taught lessons - maths, English, science, the humanities, a foreign language, artistic subjects, sports, maybe a vocational subject - and skills to support the lessons - writing, reading, arithmetic, how to compare and contrast, how to reference properly, how to hold a paintbrush, how to interpret music. What you're often not taught is how to be confident.

Interpersonal skills are learnt through interactions - the interpretation and implementation of manners, interplay with other children in the playground, family dinner time discussions, having to debate and speak up in class. Often though, you're not taught about discovering who you are as an individual. It is kind of assumed that's what parents will do, but if they don't know this about themselves, or, if they have children that are very different to them, have we [read society] ever given them the skills to deepen their children's self-awareness?

You may be given a label - shy, nerdy, swot, jock, princess, popular, fun, diva, joker, loud, academic, sporty, social, awkward - but are these really descriptions of who you are? Are you actually shy, or are you an introvert who prefers to get your energy from solo pursuits? Are you actually loud or have you associated getting some sort of praise or recognition when you're loud, so this is, therefore, the behaviour you have decided to make prominent? If you don't have an understanding of who you are, it is difficult to have the right strategies to ensure you're always at your optimum.

Confidence could be argued to be the thing that is needed to make any of the skills and learnings from school, college, university and/or work, effective. Thinking about Clance and Imes's original research on imposter syndrome[7], they found that highly qualified women doubted their ability, feeling like frauds because they didn't believe in themselves or their accomplishments. Learning and acquiring skills, even when backed up with qualifications, experience, and accolades, was not enough. These amazingly accomplished women hadn't internalised the feelings of success, and while these accomplishments remained external to them, they could discount them as not being real. Without confidence, you don't use the skills you have acquired fully. You don't explore, and you don't continue to learn by making mistakes, by making masterpieces, by accepting that both and everything in between is part of the messiness of becoming a master of your skillset. You don't believe enough in yourself to fully meet and accept where you are and where you want to go.

I believe confidence is a skill, and like any skill, it needs to be worked on to remain strong. Like with any skill, whether it's playing a musical instrument, or learning a language, or cultivating a positive mental attitude, how do you expect to get good at having confidence or being confident if you don't practice? If you think of confidence as something you have or not, and it's just down to good luck if you have it, then you can easily resign yourself to never being confident. But if you can think of it as a skill, like any skill it can be learnt, practiced, developed and honed.

Yes, it may appear that some individuals are more 'naturally' confident and as I've mentioned there is a genetic link with confidence levels, but this only makes up part of the equation. It may also be impacted by your upbringing and whether you were told you were amazing, or that you weren't good, at something. Or there may have been a more unconscious message that your parents weren't confident and confidence is associated with someone who is arrogant and bolshy, so being non-confident is a good thing. Or you may have been bullied at school, and your confidence waned, or you had a teacher that totally believed in you and built your confidence up. However, for any of these, it is about how you feel that determines your level of confidence. I think this is a good thing as it means you also have the ability to improve your inner confidence.

You can learn and appreciate what makes you tick and then use this to your advantage. Not a people person? That's okay!

You'll need to interact with people, that's life, but if you know it isn't your favourite thing, you can ensure you reward yourself with something you like doing, some downtime, or playing the guitar, or whatever it is that lights you up, as your reward. You can choose careers that are more about you as an individual, rather than having to work collaboratively. Or maybe you love interacting with small groups, but you know that it will drain you, so you need to ensure a good night's sleep beforehand and then plan your evening after to have a relaxing soak in the bath, a good book and an early night.

So how do you start improving your confidence? Take action towards your goal, no matter how small. Then take another. Then another. This is how you school yourself in the art and science of confidence. Sometimes you'll be 'successful' in as much as you will achieve what you set out to do. However, I believe all action leads to success as you'll learn something if you let yourself. Maybe you'll need to course-correct, maybe you'll need to develop a new skill, maybe you'll realise you have an unrealistic expectation, and something will take longer than you first thought. It doesn't matter - just celebrate that you took some action, you survived, and you'll take further action. You're building your inner resourcefulness. You're showing yourself that you can do this. You're overcoming any hesitancy from that voice that raises doubt. You're moving forward - moving towards where you want to be, even if the path ends up a little more zig-zaggedy than you first thought! Every action is a triumph. Every action is taking you somewhere new. Every action is building your confidence.

## EXERCISES TO BUILD YOUR CONFIDENCE

Confidence is an important attribute linked to success for many reasons ranging from improving communication and decision-making skills to being comfortable enough to show up as your true, authentic self, having faith in your opinions, and not fearing judgement from others. If you want ways to improve your self-confidence, doing these following exercises, and continuing to constantly check in on your thoughts, feelings, and actions to keep making progress will mean your confidence will [continue to] grow over time.

### *EXERCISE 1 - DO A POSITIVE STOCKTAKE*

A positive stocktake is when you take a couple of minutes to think about your day and focus on at least one thing that has gone well. Maybe you:

- like how you let someone out at the junction in rush hour
- appreciate that you went to the gym even though you really didn't feel like it
- acknowledge that you got out of bed on time and didn't hit the snooze button

- love that you were super focused on a task
- feel accomplished because you left on time for date night

Training yourself to focus on the positives means, over time, you'll start to see more and more positives easier. By appreciating all the great things that are happening in your life, it allows you to increase your feelings of self-love and self-worth, which increases your confidence in yourself.

### EXERCISE 2 - ACT 'AS IF'

This idea is from Amy Cuddy's Ted Talk 'Your body language may shape who you are'.[8]

Think about someone who you consider to be confident. Think about how they stand, how they sit, how they move, their facial expressions - and now start doing the same!

Maybe you need to:

- hold your head a little higher
- straighten your posture
- breathe from your stomach
- take a breath before speaking
- slow down your pace
- move more
- move less
- smile

Acting 'as if' you are confident starts to fool your brain into thinking and feeling that you are more confident.

When you feel confident, it comes through in your actions, so in this exercise, you're just switching the process on its head and starting with the actions to help with the feelings of confidence!

"Wait," I hear you say, "Surely by doing this, I am actually being an imposter?" Not at all! This is still you, you're still doing all the actions, but you're giving yourself some additional support. You're accepting your current state, or thought process isn't helpful to you at this moment and you're deciding to change this to help yourself. If you had a headache, you would take a painkiller, so if you're having a less than desirable response or thought, take a remedy that will help, such as a different thought or action.

Remember, you don't always have to feel a particular way to act in a particular way. Every time you step outside your comfort zone, it grows a bit until one day when you do the action that's currently causing you concern, you realise it's now actually within your comfort zone!

Your habit has been to feel and think in a certain way, and now you're training yourself to feel and think in a different way. It takes time. But when you consider that when you're feeling and thinking that you're an imposter, it's actually not true, then in many ways this is the act, and you're helping yourself to get into your natural state of being quietly confident in who you are as a person and how you show up in the world.

Also, by acting in a certain way, your thoughts and feelings will eventually catch up. Are you not convinced? Look down, slump your shoulders, downturn your mouth, think about black rain clouds. You generally won't feel very happy! Shake this off, and now sit up straight, hold your head high, look up slightly, smile, breathe deeply and think about someone you love. Do you feel that shift in energy? You moved and acted differently and physically affected how you felt. You can take control of your actions, and your thoughts and feelings will be affected. Act confidently, and think confident thoughts, and eventually, you will feel confident as well.

## EXERCISE 3 - FOCUS ON SOMEONE ELSE

I saw one of my personal idols, Marie Forleo[9], host of Marie TV, when she was touring to promote her book, 'Everything is Figureoutable', and I've unashamedly stolen this idea from her talk!

When your confidence has disappeared, focus fully on someone else and find something positive to say to them. Maybe you tell:

- a colleague that you appreciate the way they always include you
- a stranger that you love their style

- your partner that you love them for being them
- a friend how thoughtful you think they are
- your mum she is a role model for you

Be genuine and really feel what you are saying to the person. This does a few things. Firstly, if you're focusing fully on someone else, your brain has no room for negative self-talk or self-doubt. Secondly, you're not putting any pressure on yourself to change your current thinking about yourself, and are just needing to redirect all your energy to see the good in others. Thirdly, if you're noticing something positive in someone else, this is something you have to recognise in yourself as well.

I know I have covered this already in this book, but read that last point again because it is important! For you to know something, you have had to experience it yourself. So, to genuinely know something about someone else, to be able to comment on it, at some point in your life, you too have experienced this amazing quality. Knowing this can help you rebuild your own confidence.

# CHAPTER 6 - TUNING INTO YOUR INNER VOICE

"I can't believe you did that! You're such an idiot! I knew you weren't ready to take on such a large project. You're so inexperienced, no wonder you got it so wrong! No-one will ever take you seriously again. Your career is in tatters, and I'm not surprised - you are useless. Your colleagues are now all looking at you with pity, and you know they're talking about you behind your back. You're sh*t at your job, and now everyone knows it! I'm so disappointed in you."

Woah! That is some hateful dialogue and reading this I know the advice I would give to the person on the receiving end - you need to get away from this bully. It isn't acceptable, it isn't right, and you deserve better.

But what happens when that voice is inside your own head? How do you break out of an abusive relationship, when the abuser is you?

You might be reading this and feel this is too strong and that this is just what everyone does, or being self-critical keeps you motivated to achieve more, or will stop you from becoming big-headed. I want you to stop for a second and think about this though: If it's not okay to say to someone else, it's not okay to say to yourself.

The relationship you have with yourself is the most important relationship you have. You're with yourself all the time - 24 hours a day, 365 days a year. Words have power. Be honest, if someone told you someone was saying the things you're saying to yourself to them, what advice would you give them? Would you point out the other person was being unfair? Would you give them permission to make mistakes? Would you remind them of the positive things they have achieved?

Self-critical thoughts are natural, but when they are constant, they are dangerous. It can make you more susceptible to depression, anxiety, and low self-esteem. What actually makes you feel better about yourself - words of kindness or words of criticism?

Starting to become aware of your inner voice is important because your mind is constantly chattering at you, and these thoughts are going unmonitored most of the time. It isn't to judge or to further condemn yourself, but you can't change something you're not aware of, so the first step is to create that awareness, to start to catch the words you're saying to yourself, and the tone you're using.

I first became aware of my inner voice when I dropped a pen one day, and I said to myself, with such venom, "You're so stupid". Once I was tuned into this inner voice, I caught myself saying this, A LOT, in many situations - from tripping on the pavement to forgetting to call my parents one evening, to looking for my house keys that were in my hand. What effect do you think this had on me?

So, what do you catch yourself saying when you do something 'wrong', or when you dream big, or think about trying something new and exciting:

- "I'm too old."
- "I'm too stupid."
- "I'm too young."
- "I'm too sensible."
- "I'm too irresponsible."
- "I don't have enough money."
- "People will laugh at me."
- "Who do I think I am?"
- "I'm not worthy."
- "I couldn't possibly do that."
- "I'm a failure."
- "I tried before, and it didn't work."
- "I can't at the moment because…"
- "When I'm fitter/richer/slimmer, I can…"

- "I'm an idiot."
- "I'm too fat."
- "I'm too skinny."
- "I'm not experienced enough."

These seemingly 'innocent' statements said over and over can seriously start to dent your confidence, and build a story about yourself in your own mind. For example, if I'm continuously saying "You are stupid" to myself, when I want to start a new course, my story could be that I'm not clever enough so there is no point in trying as I'll never keep up. Or maybe I achieve a promotion and then start to doubt my own suitability to do the role, feeling inadequate and intellectually inferior.

And are these stories even true? Using my example, does dropping my pen make me stupid? Maybe slightly clumsy in that instance, but stupid? How many times are you holding yourself back because you have constructed a story, that you may not even be [consciously] aware of, that isn't actually even true for you?

Just becoming aware, meant I reduced the number of times I said it - or when I did, I could ask "is that true?" and if it wasn't, to change what I was saying into something positive. For example:

- "I'm not perfect, but I'm doing the best I can."
- "I meet myself where I am now."

- "I forgive myself."
- "I love myself."

Or, for those times I did feel stupid, "I feel stupid" but instead of making it part of who I am, I'm accepting it's a feeling that will go and change over time as all feelings do. Using 'I' instead of 'you' is also important because it means I can associate into the statements, and I'm not pointing a judgmental finger.

Do you feel different reading the above statements compared to the previous ones? I know I feel different hearing them!

## EXERCISE - CHANGE YOUR INNER VOICE

This is a neuro-linguistic programming (NLP) technique to try when you notice the self-doubt and deciding to change the content of the inner voice is a step too far for you at this stage.

Imagine the words are being said by Mickey Mouse*. Make the voice higher pitched and squeaky. Now take this new voice saying the old words and turn the volume down, so the comic voice is now very quiet as it's saying the words. Notice how you feel in yourself. You may notice that the words lose power when they are being spoken by a different voice. You may notice that when they are spoken quietly, you can ignore them. You may notice that you're actually laughing as you do this exercise.

There are no right or wrongs to this. It's just an experiment to see if without trying to change the words, you can change the meaning to you through changing dimensions of your inner voice.

*I use Mickey Mouse because I love Disney, but you can use any character that would work for you in this exercise.

## Catastrophising

I think one of the most damaging forms of story-telling is catastrophising - where you project out what could happen and focus on the [possible] extreme negatives. For example, you want to study a course with the aspiration that it may lead to a future career change. When you think about applying to the college, you wonder if you have what it takes, and start questioning why you think you're worthy of investing in yourself. You know you won't be able to cope with the workloads, and it will put too much pressure on your home life. You will lose friends because you'll have no spare time for catch-ups. Even if you pass the course, you won't get a very good grade so won't be able to change careers so all the sacrifices would be for nothing anyway... This story means you could talk yourself out of taking a course that you may actually love learning about.

Examine your thoughts. Would something like the following be a better story to tell yourself?

"I've spent years honing my skills and gaining experience. I have many transferable skills, including time management, delegation and prioritisation. This course excites me and could lead to different opportunities in the future. There may be some sacrifices, but I have friends and family who will support me. I will learn and adapt as I go and will keep developing and improving."

When I use the sort of example above with clients, they often acknowledge that this would be a more useful story but what if they can't cope, or they make a mistake, or say or do something that is stupid? And my response is this: So what?

You're allowed to be imperfect! In fact, why do you feel that you're so special that things won't go wrong for you from time to time? How many of the best stories are rags to riches? Sometimes you need some adversity, something not going exactly to plan, to make you strive, to try harder, to improve. It can be painful to make what you perceive to be mistakes, but it's what you do with the learning from these things that are important.

Also, I would recommend checking in with yourself to see if your 'mistake' has had the impact you're telling yourself it has had. When you go home at night, do you think about all the people that you've come into contact with during the day? Do you remember the majority of your conversations or interactions? I'm guessing not, yet I would also guess that you may fixate on a particular conversation or action you've had with someone, and tell yourself that the other person thinks "I'm stupid/was cross with me because of/judged me because I said/did". I can't say with 100% certainty that the other person is not thinking these things; however, I can't say with 100% certainty that they are either.

We are all guilty of putting too much emphasis on what others [may] think and say about us - and when you think that you probably don't review many conversations you've had, why would you think people are reviewing the ones they've had with you? Do you think you're really that important to them? If the answer is an honest yes, then maybe focusing on an empowering question like "How can I improve the situation when I next meet X?" could create a more resourceful state, then focusing on the negative [past] situation that you cannot do anything about.

The above is also a useful concept to embrace and think about if you're a people pleaser. The chances are you don't like everyone you meet. Or maybe there are certain things that people do that you don't like. Why then, would you have the expectation that everyone 'should' like you and like everything that you do?

My husband once said to me that a third of the people I'll meet would like me, a third won't, and a third won't care either way. My initial thought was that I had to work on the third that didn't like me and the third that didn't care either way to make them like me, or to at least understand what I had done 'wrong' to make them not like me. But once this initial mania had passed, this is actually hugely liberating information (although not backed by any scientific or statistical analysis) because instead of having to please everyone I meet, I can concentrate on those that I really connect with. It has helped me to realise that for some people, no matter how hard I try, they won't care or won't 'get me', and that is okay as the chances are I don't really care or get them either; this means I can save two-thirds of my energy and spend this on the people and activities that do matter to me.

## *Compassion*

According to clinical psychologist Dr. Jessamy Hibberd[1], the solution to self-criticism is compassion.

Compassion isn't about going easy on yourself, but if things go wrong, it's about being kind to yourself. If you're trying something new, it's okay to be scared and to not be perfect. There is a learning curve, and this is normal. If you make a mistake, take responsibility for it. Remind yourself you're human and ask, what can you learn from the situation? You can feel upset, or disappointed, or cross, with yourself, but then let the feeling go. Ask how you can make it right and take these actions.

I think about being on an aeroplane when they give the safety briefing and say that in the event of an emergency to sort your own oxygen mask before helping others; I think the premise works here too. If you're not telling yourself good, empowering, compassionate words and stories, can you ever tell these things to others in an authentic way?

You do have a choice on how you look at things, and the stories you tell yourself. For example, you're three months into a new role at work and are feeling overwhelmed. You can choose to tell yourself that it was luck that got you through the interview. You're not worthy of the position. You'll get found out as a fraud. Someone else would be much better at the role than you. You're not good enough. You need to work harder and longer hours to try to keep on top of things.

Or you can choose to tell yourself that you have been in the role for three months and you don't know everything yet, but you're learning on a continual basis. You bring a lot to the role, and you're finding out, and are open to, how these attributes can make you even more successful. You do feel overwhelmed at the moment, but you acknowledge you are learning and doing the best you can. You can commit to discussing workloads and priorities with your manager, and continue to work hard and be productive in the hours you designate to work each day.

Which of these stories would be more useful to you? Which one is going to help you be more resourceful, to feel better, and help you show up fully in the career you love?

## EXERCISE - TAKE ACCOUNTABILITY, NOT BLAME

As someone struggling with imposter syndrome you're likely to easily take accountability for when things go wrong, or you feel you could have done better, but you may do this from a place of blame - you feel you're not good enough and are blaming yourself for the situation.

When things don't go according to plan, try to be objective. If the report you submitted was not up to standard, was it because you hadn't prepared enough, or you had underestimated the time it would take to complete? Or maybe you had competing priorities or too much other work on? Or did you self-sabotage by going out instead of finishing the work? This isn't about blame. It is about understanding the facts. Once you know this, you can then decide what the lessons you can learn from this experience are, to then improve for next time. Take accountability for the parts that were about you but be kind and accept you are human. Also, accept any parts that weren't due to you.

Doing this exercise supports a growth mindset of continuous improvement. It helps you stop making this part of your identity as you're looking at the whole situation and choosing to see it as a learning opportunity. It isn't that you're not good enough, or you're incompetent, it is about understanding all the reasons the outcome wasn't what you had hoped for, and finding what you would do differently next time. (By the way, this also works great when evaluating what has gone well and deciding what you would do the same next time!)

## *Negativity bias*

Why is it so much easier to accept something negative that's said about you compared to something positive?

I attended a 'Secrets of Hypnosis' weekend with Richard Bandler and Paul McKenna. Whilst there, I got to know another participant, and they gave me some lovely feedback - however, I dismissed the compliments.

Some of these remarks were in direct contrast to things I'd been told at school. Yet, I found it easier to hold onto these old and outdated comments and beliefs about myself from people that are no longer in my life, have probably never thought twice about the comments made, and from people that definitely don't know me as I am today, than to believe and accept the comments from a person who had interacted with me and was generous enough to share their views.

It's actually very rude and arrogant of me to have dismissed their kind words. They were offering their opinion [of me], and although I have every right to believe, or not believe their words, by definition their opinion can't be wrong, it can just be different to mine. By offering me their opinion, they were offering me a gift. They were freely giving me [positive] feedback, and the polite response would have been "thank you", even if my underlying thoughts were that I didn't agree with them. I'm sure this would have made them feel better or more appreciated compared to my rebuttals. I may also have felt better! By arguing with their opinion, I had to recall events that I thought disproved their comments - these are things that have happened but may no longer be true, or may be things I've learnt from, but I was just taking myself back to the negative event and reliving it.

I can easily recall finding school photos where bullies had disfigured my image. I still feel like I'm not a good enough friend at times based on a flippant remark made when I wouldn't go out with my best friend after school. I still refer to myself as a swot and 'goody goody' because these were labels given to me at school. Why have these become part of my identity but comments about who I am now haven't?

It is likely this is evidence of the negativity bias - that we're more 'tuned in' to negative comments and thoughts. Even if we receive negative and positive comments with the same intensity, research suggests that the negative has more effect on our psychological state than positive comments.

You can probably think of your own examples that 'prove' your negativity bias. For example, have you ever had a fantastic day with a friend, and they make one comment you didn't like, and when you recall the day you spend more time fixated on the comment and potential meaning, rather than the positive aspects of the rest of the day? Or maybe you have received a large bonus at work, but when you check your payslip you see the tax taken; you then focus on the unfairness of the tax rather than the recognition of your work by receiving the bonus [and the amount you have actually received into your bank account]?

If it's in your biology and chemistry to be predispositioned to negativity, how do you overcome it? Becoming mindful of the stories you're telling yourself about your situation is key. When you catch yourself going into a 'woe is me' moment, evaluate what you're saying. Is it actually true? What is an objective view of the situation?

Catching your thoughts and stories and trying to put an objective filter on them gives options for how you see any given situation. It isn't necessarily about changing how you feel, but giving yourself choices - it could mean X, but it may also mean Y. Instead of just having the negative bias and reacting off of this in an unconscious way, you have a different view to consider and can then form a reaction in a conscious way.

For me, instead of thinking that the person paying me a compliment is just being nice, or finding something to say to me, objectively, maybe they are just expressing how they are feeling at this point in time. Maybe their sole intention was to share this with me. Maybe they were being nice, but they didn't have to be.

### *Being realistic but fair*

If you're struggling with imposter syndrome, it can be really difficult to be objective. I would guess you've read all or part of this book and thought "that doesn't apply to me because I really am no good at X/have fooled everyone into thinking I'm better than I am/<insert your own inner voice's reasoning for why you genuinely are an imposter>".

I do believe a positive attitude is important, but I don't believe in Pollyanna thinking that has no substance behind it. There are exercises at the end of this chapter that will build your own evidence bank of why you are great, but I also appreciate there may be times that you will need more experience, or training, or a particular skill to be able to do something well.

A question I would suggest asking yourself is: "When I think about my ideal situation, where I know I wouldn't feel like an imposter I will be..."

However, I acknowledge there can be a fine, and sometimes murky line between holding yourself back with a self-limiting belief and actually needing to achieve a particular 'level' before progressing. This is when I would suggest you get advice from someone you trust, such as a friend, a colleague, your manager, a mentor or a coach, depending on the situation. They can help you see your strengths, and their experience will also help you identify any genuine gaps.

Once you know these, you can then create a plan on how to address them.

You need to be aware of any perfectionist tendencies you may have as well. I know when I was training to become a coach, there was always one more qualification or training course I needed to complete before I would feel ready to start a coaching practice. These additional courses and qualifications do make me a better coach, I don't dispute, but they weren't necessary for me to start coaching. My own imposter told me I wasn't a coach until I was qualified to the nth degree, but the reality is until you start using your skills, everything is theoretical. It's showing up and using the techniques, and then having the supervision to reflect on my own practice that means I keep improving. Once I started, I could keep learning and adding to my coaching tool kit, but I needed to start, and to stop hiding behind not feeling ready.

I've said it before, and I'll say it again throughout this book, but doing things, and pushing yourself outside your existing comfort zone is what builds your confidence. I walk my talk, and I still push myself outside my comfort zone boundaries on a regular basis. I wish there was a magic wand that I could waft over you and 'abracadabra' you feel confident and competent. I wish there was a pill I could give you that takes away your self-doubt. Truth bomb alert - changing your inner world, by which I mean your inner voice, takes consistent work and effort. I'm sorry if this wasn't what you were hoping to read when you picked up this book, but I honestly believe that if you want to overcome feelings of being an imposter, and you want to quieten the self-doubt, you need to do the work on a consistent and continual basis to make this happen. Sometimes this work will include needing to learn a particular skill, but sometimes it is about working on your mindset and deciding to take action from where you are now.

## EXERCISE - QUIET THE SELF-DOUBT

This exercise will help you deepen your self-awareness by helping you shine a light on your habitual thoughts and inner voice. As you work through these steps, be compassionate with yourself - you'll be challenging your self-criticism with your own contradictory evidence and creating more resourceful [evidence-based] thoughts that will quieten your own inner critic and help you to build your confidence.

Give yourself time to really think about and reflect, and then, using your journal, write your answers to the following: -

1. Without judgement, write down all the negative things you say to yourself.

2. Review the list and highlight the extremes. For example, do you hear yourself saying things like "I'm **always** late", "I could **never** do that", "**All** my efforts go to waste"?

3. Now ask "Is that really true?" Cross through the negative self-talk if you can give an example that disproves the

extreme. For example, have you got an example of when you were on time? At least once did you make a doctor's appointment/school pick up/drop off/catch up with a friend on time? Have you achieved something in your life? Has there ever been a time when your efforts were recognised?

You only need to have achieved something once to be able to smash through your extreme thinking.

4. Write down all your past achievements (and then internalise these!). Review your strengths from the exercise in Chapter 3 and build on this. Think about the compliments you have received. Think about everything you have achieved - big and small. Assuming no impairment, you can probably walk, talk, read, write, text, use a computer, drive. But at some stage, you couldn't do these things. When you were learning you obviously didn't stop, because you can now do them. You persevered. You got knocked down, but you got up again (nothing's going to keep you down - thank you Chumbawamba!) You kept going until you reached your goal. And then you probably went past that - you learnt to run and jump and skate and cycle, your vocabulary increased, you could drive on motorways, you wrote essays, board presentations, and keynote speeches, you can show your parents how to use technology to keep in contact with you. Things you take for granted now were once huge tasks. You have achieved so much already.

When you review all your accomplishments, you have your

own evidence that you're capable, competent, resilient and resourceful in a variety of situations. Things may not have been perfect, or they may have taken a few attempts, but you got there. In the future, you'll confront different situations, but know that everything has a learning curve. Things may be difficult for a bit, but you now have your own evidence that you can ride this out, that it will become easier, and you can achieve. It might be time to readjust your thinking to take all of this into account and feel confident in who you are, what you have achieved and what you can achieve in the future based on this evidence.

5. Now go back to your list of negative thoughts from step 1 and cross through any that are now disproved by your past achievements. For example, if you think you're not good enough, do you have a client testimonial or comment that thanks you for your service and how you have helped them? Have you passed a test at any point in your life?

6. Review the negative self-talk you have struck through. You can now change this self-talk to something that's more empowering and true. For example, "I'm a busy person and am making an effort to be on time for important meetings"; "This task is challenging, but I've overcome bigger obstacles so know I have the ability to achieve this too"; "Sometimes people may not recognise my efforts, but I do know I'm making a difference and what I'm doing is important."

7. For any remaining negative self-talk items that you have

not struck through, can you rewrite or re-phrase any of them to use the word 'yet'? For example, "I can't do this", could be re-written as "I can't do this yet"; or "I'm so rubbish" could be rephrased to "I don't feel great about this yet".

This final step moves you from a fixed mindset of having a fact of "I can't do this" to a growth mindset where you have opened yourself up to the possibility that things could potentially change in the future.

## CHAPTER 7 - HOW TO BELIEVE IN YOURSELF AGAIN

I work with amazing, successful, talented women. However, when we start working together, they haven't just lost their spark, they have fizzled out entirely and often can't remember a time they felt confident, amazing, or even just adequate.

Believing in yourself is like a muscle, and for those of us that have self-doubt, it does need regular exercise! This is why this chapter is devoted to ideas, exercises, experiences and case studies that will challenge your thinking and help you build yourself back up again. I want you to start seeing yourself as others do, to feel the love for yourself that others feel for you, and to believe what I believe, that you're uniquely awesome, just the way you are!

### *Realise there will always be someone who is better than you*

If you only measure yourself against external recognition, the harsh reality of life is that there'll always be someone who is better than you, if not today, then in the future. Even when you reach the highest position or achieve the most prestigious award within your chosen field, the next day, week, month, year, someone else will make a better film, run a faster time, make more money, be the top author, be promoted, win your award. The bar is always being raised. However, this doesn't take away from your achievements, and it doesn't lessen your success.

You are unique, and you have your own contributions, skills, experiences, and ways of seeing the world. You're here for a purpose, and you're allowed to shine bright. Remember, there isn't one star in the sky, and I would argue it's the beauty of many that outshine the beauty of one.

Striving to be the best is not a bad thing, but holding too tightly to an unachievable outcome, I believe, is. If you achieve successes, as I've advocated throughout this book, celebrate them. Acknowledge what you've accomplished, take the accolades, let them really sink in so you can appreciate how awesome you are. Internalise that feeling and forever hold onto it so you can call on it when you need a reminder that you are amazing. You have control over this. You also have control over setting your own personal goals and trying to better yourself or to remain the best you can be in your chosen area. What you don't have control over is how you 'measure up' against everyone else as there are way too many variables outside of your control. For example, if you're going for a job interview, preparation is key. You can research the company and interviewers. You can practice the examples you'll share to demonstrate your experience and skills. You can visualise the interview going well. You can be authentic, enthusiastic and professional in the interview. These are all things within your control (and things I definitely encourage you to do!). What you can't control is if the interviewer will appreciate your examples or if another candidate is a better match for the company. You can give the very best interview you can, but there isn't a guarantee you will achieve the outcome you desire of the new job. However, if you can accept what is within your control and develop and improve within this, you can feel proud of what you're doing and achieving, regardless of the outcome.

I'm not a huge fan of comparisons as we're all different and unique - two people watching the same film will experience it differently because of things that have happened to them, their interpretations, their education, their beliefs - these all impact on how you view and experience everything. Yet, in life, you spend your time comparing yourself to others based on external measures - to the person that got the job, to the person who got the higher grade, to the person who has the smaller waistline - not appreciating that they have had a different journey to yours, not necessarily better or worse, just different. And the chances are their goals aren't the same as yours anyway!

Steven Pressfield, in 'The War of Art'[1] talks about social and territorial hierarchies. In a professional sense, we use job roles as social hierarchies - for example, the CEO is higher than directors; directors are higher than managers, etc. The same can be true in life in terms of 'life expectations' - the 'expectation' to go to university, start a career, progress up the career ladder, buy a house, have a child, own possessions, have financial freedom through savings and investments. These are all 'steps' within the social hierarchies that are created around us. The problem with this though, is your 'place' in the world is always relational to someone/everyone else's. For example, when you achieve the promotion, you have 'beat' someone else to the coveted position. You then can fall into the trap of feeling successful because you have elevated yourself in the social hierarchy, rather than feeling successful because you have achieved your own goal, or know you can add value, or that this role will make you happy.

Conversely, Pressfield talks about territorial hierarchies as your focus on the areas in life which put you in 'flow' - the things that make you happy and you can lose yourself in. It's not dependent on someone else's view of success. It's the development of skills through your own 'territorial' or internal map. This can be different for everyone, and will develop and change over time, which is great as it means there's no competition! There are no limitations other than the effort and time you can put into your position within your own hierarchy as you're choosing the targets and 'levels' you want to achieve and are happy to progress to.

I do think it's a positive thing to aspire to be great - to have amazing role models and want to achieve similar (or exceed their) accomplishments, if this inspires you and makes your heart sing. I also think it is important to accept you will do things differently to them and your journey won't be identical to theirs - it may take longer, it may be shorter, it may have a few additional stops along the way. All this is okay as it's your journey, and you'll be learning and developing as you progress along your path. I encourage you to dream big. However, I also encourage you to have a plan of how to get there and to meet yourself where you are at the moment.

I once heard this great analogy - if you're starting out as a filmmaker, don't measure yourself against Star Wars. If you feel that you need to measure yourself, measure yourself against George Lucas' first works - when he was where you are now. You need to be kind to yourself. To develop skills, whether that's learning to walk, speak, eat for yourself, becoming an amazing manager, completing your first project, writing a dissertation, running a marathon, decorating a room - whatever you're trying to accomplish - you're not born knowing this stuff, and it takes time, practice and patience to develop the skills. Why do you feel as an adult you should know this stuff or be better than you currently are, especially if you have never done something before? When you feel the need to compare yourself to someone else, just remember they're further along in this particular journey than you, and at some point, they would've been where you are now.

You have a finite amount of time on this planet, and generally, you don't know how long that will be. You can choose to spend this time comparing yourself to someone else and berating yourself as to why you're not as 'good'/'accomplished'/<insert what is important to you here> or you can choose to spend your time:

- deciding what you want to achieve
- trying to be better than you were yesterday
- finding the things that put you into 'flow' and make you happy
- improving in the areas that are important to you - whether that's to become a better communicator, writer, musician, parent, partner or something else
- finding a more fulfilling job or getting a higher-paid position, if that's what you want
- learning new skills
- challenging your own thoughts and beliefs
- experiencing life on your terms
- spending time admiring and celebrating someone else's achievements and then working out what they

did and how they did it (and, if you want to complete similar actions, in your own way, to achieve a similar result, you can choose to do this)

All this is within your control - you can decide what you want to achieve and consciously go for it. If others then don't appreciate these efforts or don't interpret them in the way you intend, that is okay - you can't control that, but you can still feel proud of your own achievements.

### *Accept you may not always win*

It sucks when you don't get what you want, but it doesn't mean you weren't worthy or right to go for the opportunity. When you try for something, and it doesn't pan out as you would have liked, what can you learn from it? After a disappointment, wait a few days and then reflect. What did you think went well? What would you definitely want to do again in the future? Is there one thing you would change next time?

I try to think about this concept in terms of the Olympics. Yes, everyone wants the Gold medal, but there is no shame in achieving the Silver or Bronze, or the fact you were good enough to be chosen to represent your country, or that you have trained so hard for so long to get to this point in your career.

### Own your luck

I hear so many clients dismissing their successes with these four words, "I just got lucky". But by using them, you're not acknowledging your achievement and potentially holding yourself in your own imposter syndrome pattern.

Maybe luck did play a part, but you did something with that luck to make your ultimate success happen. Don't believe me? Write down all the accomplishments you feel were due to luck. Next to them, write down all the things you did to take advantage of this luck which led to your success. For example, maybe you feel you got your job because you were connected to the recruiter. Yes, this is lucky; however, you would have still had to send your CV, prepare for, and show up for the interview, ask the right questions and give the responses the company was looking for, and then decide if this job was right for you. Luck may have opened the door, but you took all the actions to step through it.

Do this short activity to see for yourself how luck is, well lucky, but it's down to you what you do with that luck, and the success you achieve is a result of YOUR actions.

### Embrace change

Change is an inevitable part of our lives, yet very few of us seem to like change.

However, paradoxically, we are often all searching for a change - a change in job, a new car, a different haircut, an exciting hobby, a holiday away from our day-to-day lives. You may put a lot of thought into what you want to achieve and believe you'll be happy and confident when you do.

I think this 'I'll feel confident when...' mentality can be damaging, though. For example, maybe you believe you'll feel better about yourself when you have the perfect hairstyle. You find the perfect cut and colour for yourself, and maybe you do feel fantastic when you come out of the hairdressers. But what then? Your hair will continue to grow so if you have put your confidence into having this perfect hairstyle, what happens when it no longer looks the same? Yes, you can have it cut and coloured again, but there will be changes in between. You can choose to keep having it cut into the same style forevermore, but over time I would guess you and/or fashions will change, and you'll evolve your style.

The same is true of skills and achievements - you'll be pleased when you've achieved them, but do you think you'll never want or need to improve or learn different things or develop yourself in a new way? There isn't an end destination where you'll be this fully formed amazing individual - you're there already, and as the world changes and moves on, you have to adapt and change alongside it.

Imagine you have the perfect car for you. You have set the seat and mirrors to be in the perfect position. You have set the air conditioning to be just right. You set out on a wonderful road trip. The sun comes out - what do you do? Yup, you put the sun visor down! Oh no, it has started to rain! No worries, you put the wipers on! You're starting to feel a bit cold - just crank the heating up! You drive for hours, and it gets dark. No problem here, as you turn on your headlights!

Your car has all the tools so you can adapt and change to the circumstances around you. The car is still a car - a vehicle to get you to where you want to be, but it can have minor adaptations to effortlessly meet the different scenarios along the way. That's what I think you can cultivate in yourself - the toolkit so you can adjust to the changing situations you find yourself in, whilst remaining happy and confident in who you are along the way.

Your end goal today isn't likely to be your end goal in 10 years. Your end goal for 10 years may not even exist yet! With the pace of change, things are emerging, and ideas are forming that may mean what you want, or will become, just isn't even here yet.

If you go on a perfect holiday, do you decide you'll never go on another holiday again? If you get the job promotion to your dream job, will you remain in that job for the rest of your career? If you reach your savings goal, do you stop saving? Maybe you do for a bit. But the chances are, that even when you achieve an absolute goal, there will be another goal around the corner that you'll want to aim for. Like the seasons, you keep evolving and changing and this is just part of a process.

That's why being open to possibilities and opportunities is so important. Embrace change. Have goals but know they may change over time, and that once you've achieved one, there will be another to take its place, maybe not immediately, but eventually, because without that you won't continue to develop and learn.

This is where the adage of 'it is about the journey, not the destination' is so relevant. As I've said previously, my favourite saying is from Mahatma Gandhi, "Live as if you were to die tomorrow. Learn as if you were to live forever," and this is my guiding compass for my life. My goals are accomplished and then built on, and sometimes change and evolve as I learn stuff, but ultimately my destination is the same as everyone else's - unfortunately, death - so what is really important is the journey - how I get from where I am now, to hopefully the endpoint in a very long time, having travelled a very fulfilling route!

I don't want to force change, or to hold on so tightly to an existing situation that I'm scared for future change. The stops along the journey are important. Some I will rest at for a while, some I'll want to move on from quickly, others I may actually come back to, but this is all part of my journey. It's what is helping me to learn and grow.

I encourage you to 'go with the flow', to change and evolve, to embrace where you're at, whilst preparing for the next stage. To know you have the resources to transition as you need to. To know things are always in a state of flux, but there is beauty and excitement in that. That things don't stay the same, that sometimes things come in early, or late, or are different from how you expected, but things do change, and this is ultimately a good and necessary thing.

## CASE STUDY

I worked with a coaching client aiming for a long-term job goal and had developed a career development plan for the next five years with her. Then, one day, she asks, "What happens if I'm not happy when I get there? What if I still want more?"

My question back was "What if you do?" I would be more surprised if she didn't want more when she got there. We worked through her thinking. She had been so focused on the goal and that everything would be perfect when she achieved this, that she hadn't contemplated what would happen next. I asked, "When you achieve your ideal position, do you see yourself there until the end of your career?"

She laughed at the thought. "No, but shouldn't I then be thinking about and planning for what is next?"

"Do you know what is next?" I asked.

"No, not at the moment." We agreed to remain focused on the current plan and, when the 'next' becomes known, at some point in the future, we will focus on that then.

### *Cultivate a Positive Mental Attitude (PMA)*

As we explored in chapter 5, I believe optimism and positivity are part of being confident. I believe happiness is a state that, notwithstanding a chemical imbalance or a grief situation, you have control over. What I mean is, you can choose to be happy, or not.

I want to empower you to fully show up in your lives. To do this, you need to be in control. You need to be in control of your actions, which are pushing you towards your goals. You need to be in control of your thoughts, ensuring you believe you can achieve and succeed. You need the inner resources and resilience to overcome obstacles, and to help with this you can develop your positive self-talk. You also need to be in control of your emotions, as this will support your actions and thoughts.

So, what is happiness for you? Is it financial freedom, time with family and friends, time alone to read a book, a long run, a yoga class, a day out with your children, a weekend away with your partner, a job that you love? Or is it a feeling?

Think about when you have felt really happy. I bet you're

smiling right now! Nothing has changed in your situation, you're still sat reading this book, but you have changed your inner world. You're feeling happy because you're thinking about a happy event. You can choose to do this whenever you want!

If something negative is happening, you still have control. You can choose to sit or stand in a confident stance. You can acknowledge the situation - that it isn't pleasant/that you're uncomfortable etc. - but know this will pass. You can choose to find meaning or a different way to view the situation. You don't need to be a victim. You can take control of the only thing you ever have control over, and that is yourself.

In any situation, you'll react or have a reaction. You have a choice - you see the good, or you see the bad; you see the positive or you see the negative. Yin/yang, dark/light, day/night - everything has an opposite, and it is about the balance. Know you have a choice to see the positive over the negative, even if it takes a bit of work to begin with, you can choose to do this. And the more you do it, the more positives you will find! If you choose to see the negative, maybe you will then see more negatives - does this make you feel better?

I'm not saying to just tell yourself to be happy though. If you're caught in traffic, for example, you may feel angry or frustrated - acknowledge this, name the feeling without trying to change it - "I'm feeling cross that I didn't allow more time for this journey" - and then see what happens.

My own personal experience, and what clients often report when they do this, is that by acknowledging the emotion it then loses its power, and you can let it go. When you try to change a negative feeling, you have to focus on the emotion you don't want, and even though you're trying to make the situation better, you're still fuelling your current state. Instead, focus on what you would like to be feeling instead - maybe calm and in control. I then try to think of what I do have influence over and ask more useful questions of myself:

- "Can I pull over and let someone know that I will be late?"
- "What is the lesson in this?"
- "Why was I so cross?"
- "Is there another way I can view this situation?"

Different questions mean you get different perspectives. You go into a resourceful state, rather than just letting the frustration or anger or whatever the emotion is, keep bubbling away, growing and intensifying. You acknowledge the situation as it is and then can move on.

Personal development work is a journey, and it isn't always easy. Your emotions fire quickly and can hijack you. But becoming more self-aware, acknowledging when this happens, asking empowering questions that change perspective and/or deepen your own self-understanding will help you gain control quicker and choose to move to a more resourceful state.

For me, it's about seeing the world in a different, more positive way that leads to happiness; I contribute to my own inner confidence because I am actively developing faith in myself and the world around me.

A simple technique I use with clients is to increase their self-awareness of when they experience negativity. You can do this in a couple of ways, for example, you can wear an elastic band and every time you notice you have a negative thought, you 'ping' it on your wrist; or you can carry a notepad and write down your negative thoughts for a week. As you found in the previous chapter, it can be difficult to tune into your thoughts as they're happening all the time, but commit to be curious and non-judgemental about yourself - this is just about tuning into any negativity you may have, but it's expanding it from just the negative self-talk you have about yourself, to general negativity you may be fostering unconsciously.

For example, you may catch yourself thinking:

- "I'm so stupid."
- "Of course the traffic light would turn red as I get there."
- "Why did they email me about this and not just pick up the phone?"

- "Arrgh, it's raining again."
- "I can't believe my boss has given me this report to do by tomorrow. I can't get to the gym tonight now."

As I've said before, words are powerful. If you're having consistent negative thoughts, you're likely to be focusing on the negatives rather than the positives of a situation. By being curious, you're gently bringing awareness to your own thoughts that may now be habitual. Once you're aware of them, you can then decide what you want to do about them.

If you decide you want to see things more positively, I suggest you try this activity from success coach, Jen Sincero[2]. Every day reflect on something that has happened to you and say 'this is good because…' Choose things that were excellent, that were awful, that were just the day-to-day life admin tasks. What you're doing is training yourself to see the positive in every situation, and be grateful for everything you have.

For example:

- "I got a promotion today! This is good because I'm ready for more responsibility and will love spending the additional money."
- "I had a car crash today. This is good because no-one was hurt and I've already contacted my insurer to get things sorted."
- "My electricity bill arrived in the post today. This is

good because I value being able to use electricity in my home."

My own personal example was when our boiler broke one year on the 30th of December, and we had no heating or hot water. This was very inconvenient, but I chose to see the positives in this situation. My first grateful moment was that we maintained boiler cover, so an engineer came out on New Year's Eve.

The engineer arrived, and it was found that our heating exchange had cracked - this wasn't good news, and the engineer couldn't fix it. He put a big 'Danger, do not use' sign on our boiler. The engineer told me that I was really unlucky because this is a manufacturer malfunction and he had never seen it in this make and model of boiler before. In my head, I chose to disagree with him: I am lucky. My second grateful moment was still having all the paperwork to prove the boiler was under warranty. The engineer arranged for the part that was required to be ordered, and the boiler was fixed on the 2nd of January. My third grateful moment was that we were going to friends for New Year's Eve, so we didn't have to change any party plans. My fourth grateful moment was being able to have a hot shower at our friends' house as we were staying over. My fifth grateful moment was that it happened in a year where it hadn't been that cold. My sixth grateful moment was for our portable heaters we could bring in from the shed. My seventh grateful moment was remembering that I have a home, a roof over my head, water, and food. My eighth grateful moment was after the boiler was fixed and I had hot running water for a shower in my own home again!

The situation is the situation. I decided to control my thoughts around this and chose to see the good. This ultimately made me happier than if I decided to focus on the negatives and feel sorry for myself. Yes, I was happy when the boiler was fixed. Yes, it was inconvenient for the four days we didn't have a working boiler, but I chose to be happy in the in-between time by focusing on the positives.

**EXERCISE - BE GRATEFUL**

*PART 1*

List everything you're grateful for. I mean everything. Oxygen so you can breathe, water so you can keep hydrated, food so you're not hungry, your feet so you can walk, shoes to keep your feet warm, your eyes so you can read this book, your heart beating so you're alive, your friends and family, your computer, your phone, a hot shower, a warm bed, a home, a job, an income, books, a cup of tea - everything and anything that you have in your life that maybe you have taken for granted, but without them, your life would be worse - and say thank you! Read your list and wonder at how much amazingness is in your life already.

## PART 2

My additional challenge to you, if you choose to accept it, is for the next 66 days:

- Every morning or evening write down at least three things you're thankful for
- If something happens during the day that makes you smile, say a 'thank you' in your mind [or out loud]
- If you're going to say something negative, and you catch yourself in time, choose to say nothing
- If there is a situation you feel negatively about, think if there is a positive way to view this - maybe there is a different perspective you can take?

The second part of the challenge is designed to help you create a habit of seeing the positives in your life. You may have heard that it takes 21 days of consistent action to form a habit but Jeremy Dean's research[3], says it takes, on average, 66 days of consistent action for something to become habitual.

# CHAPTER 8 - ALIGNING YOUR INNER AND OUTER WORLDS

In the romantic comedy film, I Feel Pretty, the main character, Renee (played by the brilliant Amy Schumer) is insecure about her looks. In true 'Big' style, she wishes that she could be attractive. Then, after a minor head injury, she wakes up and sees that she's now extremely attractive! Her confidence soars, and she goes and gets her dream job, her ideal man and has lots of amazing experiences that are only available to attractive people. She then hits her head again, and the spell is broken; she goes back to how she looked previously, and with it, her confidence disappears.

**Spoiler alert** Nothing actually changed other than how Renee saw herself. [The tagline of the film is 'change everything without changing anything' so I don't feel too bad about giving this away!]

Setting aside the superficial focus on looks, I did love the message this film is giving around how we hold ourselves back by our own thoughts, actions, and preconceptions. We limit our potential. We stop ourselves going for the job we want, or asking someone on a date, or we let our inhibitions stop us from taking the opportunities and experiences offered to us, because of what we believe to be true about ourselves. We let our own self-talk and self-doubts control our lives.

The moment Renee had self-belief, she applied for the job, she talked and flirted with the guy, she got up on stage, she expressed her opinions. She may not have always got it right, but she showed up. Fully.

When Renee had positive self-worth she held her head high, she walked with purpose, she wore the clothes she felt good in, she ignored negativity as she assumed it wasn't aimed at her, she spoke up, she thought the odds were in her favour, so she took risks. And they generally paid off!

Yes, I know, this is a film, and it is designed to give the feel-good factor. But what you say to yourself and how you view yourself does have an impact on how you show up in your life. Your thoughts control your feelings, and your feelings control your actions. Your thoughts and feelings are your inner world, and your actions are your outer world. So how do you align all of this and ensure your actions are true to your feelings and thus stop the imposter emerging?

I've touched on this concept previously, but it is important, so I'm going to go through it again. Have you ever thought about something bad that has happened to you? Have you noticed that by thinking about the event, you start to feel the same feelings again - angry, mad, sad - whatever the emotions were you felt at the time? Does this then affect your actions - maybe you're snappier with your colleagues, maybe your energy slumps?

Now think about a time when something awesome happened to you. Notice how your mood shifts in a positive way; maybe you start to smile, maybe you hold your head a little higher, maybe your back straightens, maybe you get a little twinkle in your eye!

In both these scenarios, nothing has actually happened to you - you're recalling events that have already passed, but you can feel how recalling these events can have a major influence and impact on your current emotions and actions. This is what you're doing to yourself for a lot of the time. You're putting yourself into a positive or negative state by the thoughts you're choosing to focus on.

At the beginning of the film, Renee was focusing on her looks in a negative way; she felt others perceived her as being less attractive, and this theory was proved to her by her lack of dates. After her perception changed, Renee was focusing on her looks in a positive way; she assumed everyone perceived her as gorgeous and amazing, so she felt sure men would want to talk to her. She moved from assuming the worst to assuming the best (her thoughts), so she felt pretty, which made her happy (her emotions) and her actions changed as a consequence.

At the end of chapter 5, you completed the 'Act 'as if" exercise which considers the same concept but starting with taking positive actions to affect your feelings in a positive way. I don't think it matters which way round you do this as in my experience the two are so inextricably linked, but what is important is getting these two areas aligned.

### You are a work in progress

A difficult concept for some of us to accept is that we are all a work in progress, and that includes you! Like most things I have talked about in this book, it will take practice to make changes to how you feel and act. You may start to feel more confident and then find those feelings of self-doubt return, or you behave or act in an 'old' way that you no longer want to. You're not a failure if this happens; this is normal and to be expected. It's taken a lifetime to create the person you are today, and it will take the rest of your life to create the person you're going to become. You'll have successes, and you'll have setbacks, and this is all good!

The difference is you now have so many strategies and tactics available to you that when you find yourself out of alignment, you have a wealth of ideas and exercises to change this quickly.

### *Future pace yourself*

Imagine you have been given the chance of an exciting opportunity but your inner voice is telling you, you can't do it. The fear is rising as you don't feel ready, and going for it would make you feel like an imposter because your actions are not aligned to your feelings. But there is this niggling doubt that if you don't go for it, you might regret it. What should you do?

As you now know, fear is your way of protecting yourself. Sometimes this is justified, and sometimes it isn't. A simple way of helping to realign your thinking and actions is this reframe Amber Rae shares in 'Choose Wonder Over Worry'[1], when instead of staying in the present and asking a question, such as "should I stay or move on in my current job?" go into an imaginary future and ask "do I wish I had stayed or moved on?" Putting yourself into the future state, you're giving yourself the benefit of your own wisdom, of time, of experience, of reflection. You're taking away some of the immediate angst about a decision and giving yourself the longer-term view. Listen to the answer from your future self and accept this instinctual knowledge. I know it can be scary, especially when you're unsure in the moment of how to achieve something, but as the phenomenal Marie Forleo says, "Everything is figureoutable!"

And what happens if your future self is telling you that you should stay as you are? Is this a self-limiting belief? Is it your fear? How do you know when it is genuine to not go for an opportunity?

Throughout this book, I'm empowering you to learn more about yourself and to learn to trust in yourself. This is a really tricky one to answer but remember that whenever you say yes to something, you're saying no to something else, and vice versa. So, if you're deciding to say no to the opportunity, what are you saying yes to instead? Maybe you feel that there are still opportunities to develop where you are, or you feel you can still add value. Maybe where you are suits your current lifestyle. Maybe saying no to the opportunity means you genuinely don't want the stress at the moment so are saying yes to keeping the status quo.

Deepening your self-awareness means you can start to trust in yourself and know when saying no is the right thing for you. By being aware that everything is in balance, and with a finite amount of time available, that any yes decision will mean a no somewhere else, means you can start to take a more conscious and strategic view for yourself. Maybe instead of 'no', it's learning to say 'not now' when you have weighed up what saying 'yes' would really mean you are saying 'no' to!

### Are you a tapestry?

A tapestry looks amazing on the outside, but if you turn it over, it looks messy and not like the image that's being shown to the world. Is this the current reality for you between your inner and outer worlds? On the outside, everyone sees you as complete, totally unaware that inside you're trying to work out which thread goes where, and when to tie something off and when you should go over or under the knot?

I'll let you into a secret... this is pretty much everyone's reality! Remember the examples in chapter 2 of all the celebrities and public figures that have amazing accomplishments, so on the outside have beautiful tapestry, but on the inside are plagued with self-doubt?

As discussed throughout this book, confidence in yourself isn't about the outward show. It's about the self-belief you have - it's learning that you can navigate the threads and ensure everything will come together because you know your worth and have a realistic view of your own abilities. You're cultivating a growth mindset where you know there is the potential for improvement if you want it. You accept that you have choices, whether that's over what you do, how you act (or react), and how you choose to feel. Any perceived failures suck, and they are always tough, but you can see them as learning experiences - maybe not on day one, but you are self-aware enough to know you may need some time, but you can reflect and take the positives from the situation.

As you move into the next chapter, you'll be identifying goals that are aligned to your values and motivations in all areas of your life. You know things may be or may become, challenging and you accept that self-doubt may creep back in, but you also know that you have one life and you have to try. You may not succeed, but something amazing will come out of the experience, and it's the behaviour of trying and taking action that's most important to you.

Believing this gives you permission to create and live your own big life, as defined by you!

## EXERCISE - BELIEF STACK

A different take on the 'Quiet the Self-Doubt' exercise you completed in chapter 6, is an exercise I learnt from fellow life coach Millie von Mallinckrodt-Grant[2] and that is to build a belief stack.

In your journal, write: 'I'm good enough because', and then list at least 50 reasons why this is true for you.

List all the positive beliefs about yourself; list all the experiences and skills you have that you're proud of; list all your behavioural characteristics and values that make you unique and awesome. Keep writing until you have at least 50 items on your list.

Aligning your inner and outer worlds, so you feel as confident and loved and accomplished as your external world sees you, takes consistent mindset work. This positive belief stack exercise is a way for you to build your own strong confidence foundations. You can refer back to what you've written if you need a confidence boost in the future. You can add to it over time. You can re-do the exercise in its entirety if you want. When I do this, I then find it fun to compare and contrast my list with earlier versions to see what remains the same, and what new things get added or changed over time!

# CHAPTER 9 - DEFINING YOUR BIG LIFE

I love Disney. I'm not going to justify this statement, it's just my truth, and I'm okay with this! I was listening to my favourite Disney song, 'How Far I'll Go' sung beautifully by Alessia Cara (knocking Idina Menzel's 'Let It Go' off my top spot for the best 'I'm defying everyone and following my own dreams' car karaoke song), and it got me thinking about the limitations we put on ourselves when trying to conform.

Conformity takes many shapes, whether it's a career path you think you should take - maybe because that's what your degree subject is in, maybe because everyone tells you that you will make a great teacher/manager/lawyer/<insert profession here>, maybe because you made a big thing about entering a particular profession and now don't know how to get out of it, maybe because of the money you can earn, maybe because you feel pressure to go for that promotion or next step; or a life decision you feel you should choose because the age you are at - we have all been in those situations, with the little head tilt of expectation when asked by a caring relative or friend about getting a partner/settling down/marriage/buying a house/having a child/getting a 'real' job - and you have the choice to either say what is expected - "I really want that/I haven't found the right person/job/place but I am looking" or go against the norm and state your real desires - "I'm happy doing my own thing/I can't wait to take a year out and go travelling next year/A relationship would be nice, but at the moment, I'm doing amazing things in my career and that is where my focus will be for the foreseeable future/<insert your own truth here>".

A 'job for life' is a very dated concept yet for some of us we still view our career in quite a linear way: you progress along a particular career path, seeking promotions because this is the 'norm' or what you feel is expected of you, never questioning if this is really what you want. Having spent so much time, effort and money on honing your skills and experience in a particular field or industry, why would you then throw this away to start again in a different area? If you love what you do, it's great to continue, but what if you now only feel so-so about your career choices?

I admire people that decide they want to be in a particular profession and go full out on this and progress along their chosen path for their whole career - as long as they continue to love what they do. I admire people that decide they want to be in a particular profession or achieve a particular goal, go full out on this, maybe achieve success, and then change their minds and try something else. Staying on that original path just because you're worried about your pride or what others will say because you change, is no different to staying in a relationship for the sake of the kids. No-one benefits!

There is space for specialisms; it's great when you have that moment when you realise you have found your purpose, but is it really your life purpose or your purpose for now? For example, I feel that coaching is my purpose - to help people get from where they are now to where they want to be and to feel genuinely confident doing this. However, I loved marketing when I was in a marketing role, and I loved project management when I was in a project management role. I can't even imagine some of the jobs of the future that may or may not be perfect for me. I don't think this will diminish what I can offer in coaching, but what if I do change careers and this new one then feels like my purpose?

In 2008 I ran a marathon - I trained hard for a year and achieved my goal. I no longer run long distances because I don't really like it. I'm so happy I ran a marathon, but I've absolutely no desire to run another. I know there are many people out there like me. There are also many people out there that have run multiple marathons and love it. Both are great as long as the activities are still aligned to the individual's goals and happiness levels. I've now embraced the fact that I want to collect 'experiences' and that I'll work hard on a particular goal, and, once achieved, I will be more than likely to then move onto the next. I accept I get bored easily, that I love to challenge myself and that I want to experience as much as I can in this life.

It's almost like when you fall in love, and they're 'the one' and then it doesn't work out, and your next love is 'the one' - does it mean your original feelings were wrong? Maybe, or it just means that's what you felt, and it didn't work out, or things have changed, and you have grown and evolved and are now free to love again. You can still remember the other love fondly [if you want], but you've changed.

You have dreams and ambitions for your life, but how often do you squash them because you can't see how you can make them happen, or tell yourself it isn't the right time, or, possibly the most damaging, are worried what other people will think and say about your decisions?

I hate the word 'should'. You 'should' do well at school, so you can go to university, so you can get a job that pays a lot of money. You 'should' get married, buy a house, have children. You 'should' be responsible and do what everyone else does - a job that has you dreading Mondays, a regular income, adventures only on weekends and in your two week's holidays. Society is an institution that has us believing one way is 'better' than another: that more money is better; that there is an order we 'should' do things in our life; that it's acceptable to feel stressed and always be busy because that is 'the norm'.

There is a difference between what you can do (and what you can do well) and what you want to do. You trick yourself into thinking that if you do what you're 'supposed' to do, and you do it well, that this will fulfil you. But when you have a real ambition, goal or dream to do something else, something different, this won't be quieted by doing what you 'should' do. Your conformity may mean outer peace in your life's design, but it causes you inner conflict.

Your dreams, ambitions, and goals are yours. They are beautiful, precious and totally unique to you. They light you up and give you that fire in your belly to excel. No-one but you will ever fully understand the passion you feel for them.

My nan died of Huntington's disease. She and my grandad had spent a lot of their lives planning for their retirement. Nan's illness robbed them of these plans and dreams. I think this is maybe what has galvanised me into living life on my terms, of defying the 'should's' that don't make sense to me and finding the things that make me happy and fulfilled.

I'm now going to share some of my own life experiences to show how I've defined my own big life. These will be different for you, and some of the 'should's' of society may be things you want for yourself, and this is all good! It's about making conscious decisions though, rather than sleep-walking through your life; doing things in a deliberate and intentional way, because you want to, rather than because you feel it's what is expected of you.


## CAREERS

I didn't know what I wanted to do when I left college, so I chose to start working until I figured out what I wanted to specialise in. I had thought this might take a year or two, and I would then go to university at that point. The long story short is that I worked for a large financial institution for 17 years and never actually ever figured it out! I did discover the Open University though and graduated with a Bachelor of Science Open Degree in 2014 after five years of part-time study in lots of different subject areas whilst working full-time.

When I was at college, there was a lot of pressure from lecturers for me to go to university because I had good grades. Even my friends couldn't understand why I didn't want to go, because, at the time, graduate positions were much more highly paid than non-graduate positions.

But I chose my path and didn't do what was expected.

The fantastic thing about working for a large organisation is the opportunities you can go for. I went from starting as a data-inputter, to an administrator, to working in a legal team, to working on an internal IT help desk, to being a direct marketing manager for the agricultural sector, to train as a project manager for the auto lease business, to work as a campaign coordinator within retail and finally I worked as a product manager for savings. And I loved every position I held... eventually!

Jumping business units and careers meant my experience and skills grew, but also led to feeling like an imposter for much of my career because I kept challenging myself and never felt like I had specialised in a particular area. (And these feelings led me to my current career path.)

When I chose to take voluntary redundancy in 2014, I received mixed reactions. Some colleagues and friends were pleased for me, but others let their own fear colour their reaction:

- "What if you can't get another job?"
- "I've looked, and there isn't much out there for your grade."
- "What about your pension?"
- "You should really consider your future."

These are all valid concerns, and they were things I had considered, but I also could see the opportunity I was being presented with. I enjoyed working for the organisation, but it was pretty much all I had known in terms of my working life. I had often thought of leaving, and even occasionally had applied for positions, but the 'golden handcuffs' of my situation meant it never felt the right time to go.

Taking voluntary redundancy did feel right to me though. I had inner confidence that I would be able to find another job. I had worked out that I could take a pay cut if necessary, to be able to try a different position. And even when the fears started to take over, I knew that if I didn't take the opportunity, I would regret it. So I took it.

And I never regretted it.

## BUSINESS

In July 2018, I moved to part-time hours in my 'day job' to spend more time in my coaching practice. The question I'm most asked is, "When will you be full-time in your business?"

I know this is coming from a place of support, but I feel that there is an assumption or unspoken expectation in this question - that I 'should' want to work full-time in my business and I'm not successful in business until I am working only for myself.

One day I might work full-time as a coach. But I may not. At the moment, I'm enjoying the journey. I love that I've created a portfolio career for myself. I love that I have time to devote to coaching and building my business each week, but I also love that I get to go into an office and have conversations with colleagues and use and build my other skills to support another business. I love that I can keep learning, and this can be helpful when I'm coaching small business owners. I love that I have a salaried income that supports my need for security.

Having a portfolio career does have challenges, but I don't feel that my business success is as binary as working 100% in my coaching practice or not. My business success is down to the value I add to my clients' lives and how I can support them in making the changes they want to.

## RELATIONSHIPS

When I married my amazing husband, Alex, I was 21 years old. We had been together for three years and had lived together for just over a year. I was told by many colleagues that I was too young, and it would never last.

As I went through my twenties, I was asked when we would have children. When I told people I didn't want children, I was told I would change my mind. It drove me crazy! I would never say to someone who wanted children 'you'll change your mind' so why was my decision so easily over-turned? I love children. I love being an aunt and godmother. I just knew I never wanted my own children. I'm in a caring, empathetic profession and it's often assumed I have children. I don't, and I'm okay with this. I suppose I have a 'should' that I'm imposing here - that I believe because I'm okay with this that everyone else 'should' also be okay with it!

As I've gotten older, the question of when I'm going to have children is no longer asked, but there is sometimes the 'head tilt' of not wanting to ask, but assuming that maybe I can't have children. That may or may not be the truth, but it doesn't matter. I made a decision not to, but society doesn't always feel it should honour this choice, and I sometimes feel that it sees my decision as lesser than if I had decided to become a mother.

I know myself well enough to know this isn't the path for me. I don't think I would be a good mother for many reasons. This isn't a need for reaffirmation from anyone; this is just my opinion on myself - you can have an opinion that differs, but your opinion isn't any more valid than mine.

Your experiences are your own, and what works for you, may not work for me. You can share your opinions and others will share theirs with you, but don't confuse opinions for facts. And when opinions are shared, remember you don't have to take them on board, the same way you don't need to be offended if someone decides not to take on your opinions.

## FRIENDSHIPS

I love spending time with my family and a wide circle of friends. I love my husband very much, but I know, for me, I need other people in my life to experience different things, have different conversations and share different points of view.

As an introvert, I prefer one-on-one interactions or small groups, over larger get-togethers. I value my friendships and make it a priority to maintain them. I'm proud that I'm still friends with a couple of people that I've known since I was four years old, and for one of these, I'm the godmother to her beautiful daughter! I'm still friends with some special people I went to secondary school and college with; I've stayed in touch with people I've worked and shared a connection with over the years; I love that I have friendships formed as a result of other friends, or from networking, or from burlesque, or from courses I've attended, or from holidays I've been on.

I'm not the most outgoing or charismatic individual - traits often thought of as 'should's' for attracting or keeping friends - but I am curious (or some may say nosey!) and open. I love finding out about people. I love asking questions and understanding people's views. I want my own thinking to be challenged and believe interacting with people is a way to do this. Yes, I do feel shy when I first meet new people. Yes, I do worry about what they think of me. Yes, it's an effort for me to start a conversation. Yes, it does take energy to keep in contact and arrange to meet up. Yes, there are some days it feels easier for me to do all of this than others. And yes, it's always worth it!

## I DO IT, JUST BECAUSE...

An area of my life that does flummox some individuals is that I have an 'adrenaline junkie' streak and I love learning circus skills! I went to a day workshop about ten years ago and learnt stilt walking, flying and static trapeze and juggling. The only thing I was even marginally good at was the static trapeze, but I loved trying all of it!

I then went to a weekly class to learn aerial hoop. This is tough on the back of the knees, but I loved being in the air and having that childlike freedom of trying shapes and transitions. I tried silks, but it wasn't for me. A couple of years ago, I went to a Cyr and German wheel workshop. The German wheel was my favourite, and I loved the tricks I performed [albeit with a lot of help from the instructors!]. I have my own poi and love using them in the summer, even if I seem to spend more time hitting myself in the head than making beautiful shapes! I love hula hoop, I've walked on hot coals, and at the end of March last year, I learnt how to walk (and jump) on broken glass and lay on a bed of nails.

All of these 'skills' are pretty much forgotten as soon as I walk out of the classroom. I have no intention of mastering them, but I love the experience of trying them. Experience has shown me that I'm unlikely to be naturally good at these things, but I have the confidence in myself to give them a go. I show up, I try my best, I giggle, I laugh at myself, I try some more, I feel proud that I tried, I go home, and I sleep very well!

I do this because it makes me happy. No-one else needs to understand it. I love it when a client finds the thing they do 'just because' and no longer feel the need to provide justification to others for it. This is what I want for you too - to find the things that light you up and to have the confidence to go for them, just because.


## EXERCISE - WHAT'S YOUR 'JUST BECAUSE'?

What would you love to do, for no other reason, than 'just because'?

Remember that Ceroc/pottery/French class you loved but gave up because you weren't very good? Or what about the book club/Toastmasters/yoga practice you stopped because you ended up spending your evenings working instead? Is now the right time to give yourself a few hours each week doing something you love, even if you're no good at it and there is no other purpose than to enjoy yourself?

I encourage you to broaden your horizons. Read things you wouldn't normally read. Visit new places. Try things that are outside of your comfort zone, just to see if you like them or not. Explore everything! You are a detective in your own life, on a mission to uncover all the things that you're passionate about! Along the way, you will discover so much - including the things that you don't like or even hate - and this is also important information in your own self-discovery and self-awareness journey. Doing different things, seeing different sights, reading different books and articles gives you different perspectives, different ideas, different ways to see and experience the world and a different mindset.

### You are going to die

This is a scary thought for many of us, which is probably why most of us live our lives as if we are immortal - putting off doing things because we think we will always have more time. We almost need to find a way to remind ourselves that death may be the scariest thing out there and any actions we take, even if they end in mistake, or embarrassment, or an outcome we hadn't expected, are all a lot less scary than dying and not taking any action.

Do you lack the confidence to go after your dream, or to take a particular action because you're worried about how 'society' will view you? Who determined the 'norms' you're living your life by? What if you discovered these are all illusions? Not to get all 'Matrix-y' on you, but your reality is just that - yours - and your partners, your friends, your families, everyone else's realities are their own. It is why two people can eat the same thing and have different reactions - one loves it, one hates it. Both their realities are their truth, but which one is 'the truth'? It's all about perspective.

I love this Erin Hanson quote from her stunningly raw poem 'What if you fly?':

---

"And you ask "What if I fall?" Oh, but my darling, What if you fly?"

---

And, what if you fly? At this stage, there is as much chance of flying as there is of falling - 50/50 - yet you choose to focus on the fear of falling, over the freedom of flying - even when both are equal possibilities. You can choose to put your energy into making your dreams a success, finding innovative solutions to challenges, deciding on the small steps you need to achieve to build towards your ultimate accomplishment; or you can think of all the reasons you can't do something, focus on the obstacles, procrastinate and decide to give up. I'm not saying to not be aware of risks and issues - fully understanding what you're facing puts you in the best position to overcome the difficulties that may come your way, but you can focus on how you'll overcome them, rather than seeing them as total roadblocks to your success.

You tend to overrate your chance of failure and underrate what could be the successes. But do you ever consider the failure in passivity? By doing nothing, you may think you're avoiding any failure, but is this true? Is not achieving what you really want in life a bigger failure than not trying? If you were to die in the next year, would doing nothing now seem less of a failure to you than going for your goal and maybe making some mistakes along the way? If dying is the most terrifying thing out there, surely anything you do now is going to be less scary, less risky and generally more fun?

Let's play this through. You decide not to try to go for that goal - maybe you decide that if you went for the promotion and didn't get it, it would be the worst thing in the world as everyone would think you were a failure. Doing nothing, not sending in your CV and applying means you don't have to face that future. It also means that you could be haunted by the 'what ifs'. What if I was the best person for the role? What if I look back when I'm 60 and really regret not taking the chance? What if I don't get the position, but my boss now doesn't realise I want a promotion so doesn't consider me for a new exciting project in the future either? What if I wasted an amazing opportunity? It may be that these what-ifs are not as bad for you as the what-ifs of going for the goal, but acknowledge there is a choice to be made and that simply doing nothing will also have consequences.

Eddie Cantor's quote, "It takes 20 years to make an overnight success", is a great reminder that you see the finished result of someone's hard work, but not necessarily the journey they have taken to get there.

You often give up on something because it's taking time. You may not stop to question if you had an unrealistic expectation on the time that it would take, and just assume it won't happen for you. Yes, there are the rare occasions that things don't take long and fall into place for someone, but, for the majority of situations and scenarios, things do take time. Accept there could be hurdles and challenges. Acknowledge things may not come easily, but that your goal is more important to you. This means instead of letting any setbacks damage your confidence in your ability to achieve; you realise it's part of the journey, that maybe this part does suck, but it will be worth it and that obstacles are a normal part of the process. Accept this could be the reality; hope for the easy path but keep focused on the end goal and what this means to you. Remember you can continue and you can achieve, even if it's a bit more difficult, or takes a little longer than you first had hoped for.

I really don't want you to be so scared of dying that it's an all-consuming thought, and I've not taken any religious or spiritual beliefs into account - what I'm trying to do though is to wake you up to the fact that, like everyone else, you're not immortal, yet you often spend your time, effort and lives as if you are. Just putting a little focus on your immortality, will hopefully help you to take some action to go for the things you really want to achieve and to stop putting off things for 'someday'. This might be your only shot at this life and tomorrow is not guaranteed for any of us.

We are all unique, and we all have different goals and aspira-tions. No-one has the right to judge you and your life decisions. Be proud of your journey - it's yours, and whether it's a straight path or a winding road, it's your adventure to love and cherish - I just encourage you to really live it.

## EXERCISE - DREAM BIG AND SEE HOW FAR YOU CAN GO

My challenge to you is to spend some time defining the type of life you would like. Consider all the things you have squashed over the years: What do you want to achieve in your life? What resources do you need to make this happen? What one thing can you do today to start making this a reality for you?

Please note, some things you decide on may take a long time to happen, but until you have made the conscious decision of what you want your life to look like, you can't start putting the actions in place to make it happen.

### *DREAMING BIG*

It can be difficult to dream big, especially if this is something you haven't done for a while, or maybe have never felt you have had the chance, or confidence in yourself, to do. So, if you're struggling with this exercise, some questions to consider in your journal include:

- What did you want to be when you were younger?

- If money were no object, what would you do with your time and energy?
- What activities put you in a state of 'flow'?
- What do you love doing?
- When you were a child, what did you love doing?
- If you were a colour, what colour would you be?
- If you were a shape, what shape would you be?
- What happens when you feel excited?
- What do you think your 10-year-old self would tell you to try?
- What about your 70-year-old self?

## *WHAT MORE DO YOU WANT?*

What do you want? Don't censor yourself. Write it all down.

Now, I'm telling you, you can have it. What more do you want? Keep going and list it all out. Give yourself permission to say what you really want.

I tell you again. You can have it all. What more do you want? Keep going until there is nothing else to come out.

This is a powerful exercise I do with clients as it allows you to move from what you want at a conscious level, to your deeper wants and desires, often uncovering things you may not have been aware of, or helping you to understand the 'why' or real purpose behind your want.

## *HOW FAR WILL YOU LET YOURSELF GO?*

It's great reading about this, doing the exercises, and telling yourself you can do it, but it's when you actually start doing the work that your confidence really starts to grow, the feelings of being an imposter will quieten, and you will start to believe in yourself again.

However, expect to experience an element of imposter syndrome as you're moving to something unknown and have to learn a new skill or way of being, thinking or feeling, to be successful in your next challenge. Accepting that you want to keep achieving and growing, I think the key is then to have strategies to manage these feelings:

1. Become aware and acknowledge all your feelings. Name the emotions and write them down. Sit with them. Appreciate these feelings - it may be you're trying to protect yourself. Consciously start to notice when you experience these feelings: Where does it happen and when? Is there a particular trigger? If you feel confident, when and how does this happen?

2. What is the work you need to do? Do you need to improve? Is there training/qualifications/experience you need to acquire? Do you need to carve out time in your day? Or is this about your mindset? Do you need to accept what you have achieved already? What lessons can you take from these

accomplishments to support you in changing your mindset on how you're feeling at the moment? If this was a friend, what would you say to them?

3. Journal on a regular basis. Write down your feelings but don't censor yourself - just let it flow. You'll see how getting things out will reduce the impact it has on you, and how often you run out of words, or you get to the answer you're looking for, or, when it's on paper, it just seems smaller. And, if it still does seem as big, you'll be able to review and see if there are any patterns to be aware of - triggers, clusters in the writing, etc. - you can then put plans in place to tackle each of these.

## CHAPTER 10 - STARTING TO LEAD YOUR BIG LIFE

As you've read this book, you've had so many ideas and strategies to help you overcome self-doubt, quieten the inner critic and build your confidence.

By now, you know the truth - that you are good enough. You're good enough to take a job promotion, good enough to be a mother, good enough to be accepted into a university, good enough to enrol in a dance class, good enough to learn how to paint, good enough to earn more money, good enough to do whatever it is that you've been holding yourself back from doing, being or achieving up to this point.

You may not be great when you first try something new, but you're worthy of trying. You may not succeed on your first attempt, but you're more than good enough to go for it. There may be a learning curve, and that's okay - it's normal and natural and means you're moving outside of your comfort zone and challenging yourself.

## Set yourself some honest goals

Looking at what you want, what you already have in your life, and the resilience you must have, to have got to this point, what is the one thing you can do today to start moving you towards what you want next?

I'm a fan of going after your big hairy audacious goals (BHAG) - I think you need to have goals to grow and develop, and the desire and want to achieve these is amazing. I'm also a fan of acknowledging where you are now and identifying those smaller goals that are required to help you achieve the bigger goal. Each step should be a little stretch from where you are now, so you feel like you've accomplished something when you achieve it. For example, if you decide you want to run a marathon and you're currently a non-runner, your first step might be to invest in a pair of good running shoes and to start running a half-mile a day. Once you've achieved this, you can set a goal of running a mile a day for the next seven days, and then build up. Overall, you will still achieve the goal of running 26.2 miles, but it feels far more achievable because you have met yourself where you are currently, and built from there.

## *Be kind to yourself*

As mentioned earlier in the book, it takes on average 66 days to form a habit. That's just over two months of consistent change before this change no longer requires the same level of effort.

Making changes isn't always easy, whether it's stopping a 'bad' habit, such as smoking, or starting a 'good' habit, such as regular exercise. I have tried to make positive thinking and having positive thoughts a habit, but I do find it still takes me some degree of effort. The more I do it though, the more often it's just my way of choosing to see the world. This is why people think I'm a positive person - and I love that people perceive me in this way - it's how I want to be perceived, and how I perceive myself. But it's something I work at. The same way a good driver only remains a good driver if she keeps doing all the good habits whilst in the car, or an outgoing person remains outgoing by continually talking to people in social settings. I remain positive because I choose to keep seeing the positives and verbalising what these are to people. The good news is, anyone can cultivate this attitude if they want. The bad news is that once you start, you will need to keep going to keep it up.

We are all a work in progress. You have good days, you have bad days, you have in-between days, and this is all okay. It's part of life, and it's shaping who you are. Meet yourself where you are, accept it, and then let it go and move onto focusing on where you would like to be. Don't force changes, don't berate yourself because you had a negative thought, or didn't achieve X or Y or Z, just accept that that's where you are at the moment, and focus on what you want to do next. Put plans in place and go for it - the exercise at the end of this chapter will help you do just that.

### *Find other successful people...*

...and talk to them (or read their autobiographies or blogs)! Find out how they have done what you want to do, to see if how they have achieved it can shortcut your own learning. Get their knowledge - then evaluate and take what is important to you, make this learning your own and take action. What they are saying is not perfect; it's just their truth at that moment in time. Now see if it's your truth. Has it changed your perspective in any way? Maybe it makes you think about something else/a different solution? If you don't agree with what they say, that's okay - you're allowed to have different thoughts, opinions, ideas, and ideals. But be conscious of this - think about why it worked for them, but won't work for you. Use their experience to help you achieve your goals.

### *Figure out your own motivations*

In chapter 4, we covered motivation, but I think this is the right time to share with you a different perspective. I do this because self-development work can be hard. You won't always succeed in the way that you think you will, and sometimes what you find out about yourself isn't pretty.

An interesting question posed by Eduardo Zanatta in his Ted Talk from April 2012[1] is "Which one is greater, my desire to succeed or my fear to fail?"

We all hold up our successes, and rightfully so - we have achieved something we have set out to do - but what supported our motivation in this achievement? Was it the satisfaction or personal growth or sense of accomplishment we knew we would feel, or was it that we didn't want to show up to that next appraisal, or coffee with friends, or family get together and say we hadn't achieved what we had so proudly declared as being our next big project when we last met?

I think of a desire to succeed as something you're working towards, and the fear of failure as something you're working away from. You may end up at the same point, but what is driving you are two very different motivations. One, you are focused on you - what you're trying to achieve, what this will give you, what you need to do to get there. The other is avoiding those negative feelings, thoughts, words, and reactions if you don't achieve something. Both can be extremely powerful.

I like to think I challenge myself regularly, and it's my desire to succeed at these goals that I set myself that are my motivation. This thought was challenged a couple of years ago though, when I set out to walk around the Isle of Wight - 106km/66 miles - in 24 hours. I trained hard for four months, walking up to 12 hours a day over the South Downs, on my own. I walked over 300 miles in training and was excited to take part in the event. I had raised money for charity, had told my friends, family, colleagues and social media followers. I even knew to work on strategies to support my mental resilience, knowing that there would be tough times - for example, if I walked for 12 hours and achieved 53km, I would be tired but would only be halfway there!

I set off, and it started well - I had a good pace, I chatted with fellow walkers as moral support on different parts of the journey. At 52km I could feel the blisters but thought I'd try to the next stop - this was my new tactic - just keep going to the next stop (~15-20kms) and then I could quit - although I never thought this would actually happen. At the 67km rest stop, I took my boot off to have my blisters treated - then couldn't get the boot back on because my foot swelled too much. This was not part of the plan! I lay on the floor, legs elevated, shaking and called my husband [at 2 am] to discuss strategies. His was clear - I had to stop. Mine was less clear - I could keep going with one boot on (~39km/24 miles - that was totally doable). I was not prepared to give up.

But it wasn't the feeling of success if I achieved this challenge that was spurring me on at this point, it was the fear that I wasn't going to achieve something I had told everyone I was

going to do. I had attached shame to not achieving this goal.
I cried, sobbed - and not because of the pain in my feet, but
because I had to publicly declare I had failed. I would have to
go into work on Monday, and instead of regaling everyone
with my stories of triumph, I'd have to say I hadn't done it.
My heart was so heavy. I thought I was undertaking this
challenge for myself, but the non-achievement became
attached to what everyone else would think of me. Extrapo-
lating this out, I wonder if my achievement would also have
been for others to praise me? Holding a mirror up to yourself is not always an attractive thing to do.

And what actually happened when I posted to say I had had
to retire from the event? There was an influx of amazing
messages! Some people sympathised, most congratulated me
on what I had achieved (thank you to those that pointed out I
had walked a marathon and a half, even if I didn't see this as
an achievement at the time), some even kindly sponsored me
more money! People were kinder to me than I was to myself.
In my head, they would be so disappointed in me when
really, I was just disappointed in myself.

It does still smart when I think back. But it also taught me
that sometimes the labels you attach to things - 'success',
'failure', 'good', 'bad' - are far more powerful than you realise
and influence you in both positive and negative ways. Really
understanding why you're doing something, and what you
want to achieve is important - did I want to raise money for
a good cause, or did I want to say I had walked 66 miles in 24

hours? I thought it was the former, but the reality was that for me, once I had set myself the challenge, the latter was more important than I realised.

I think setting scary goals is important for your own growth. So, dream big and go for them. Tell the world if you want to, or not, that's up to you. But make a commitment to yourself and try your hardest. But, if you give it your all, and you 'fall short', try to go gentle on yourself. What would you say to your best friend or partner? What are you saying to yourself? Be kind! They say it is better to have loved and lost than to have never loved at all - I believe it is better to have tried and not quite achieved, but have achieved something along the way than to give up before giving it a go - it's totally the same, and just as memorable a saying!

And, yes, my confidence has grown as a result of this experience - although I'm not ready, and not sure if I ever will be ready to take on that particular challenge again! But I am now proud that I walked 41 miles around the edge of the Isle of Wight. I am upset that I didn't complete the challenge, but I'm more accepting that physically this wasn't meant to be (this time). I've signed up to more [different] challenges and will train hard for them - I'm nervous in case I don't succeed again, so the fear of failure is still very real for me, but when I sign up, it's because I want to achieve something, for me. I have a lot of evidence that I've achieved other goals. I now also have evidence that even when I haven't succeeded, I have survived and I've learnt and grown from the experience.

## EXERCISE - SMART GOAL-SETTING

Goals are personal and unique to everyone - what may be satisfying or exciting for some, may be stressful or boring for others. Increasing your self-awareness throughout this book, giving yourself permission to invest in defining a life on your terms, and trusting in yourself and what you love doing is a great way to allow yourself to think about what goals you want to set for yourself next. Also, to be able to create a life that's more satisfying and aligned to your definition of a 'big life'.

Making changes can be difficult, so I would encourage you to concentrate on one larger goal at a time. The following are five steps to help you achieve your goals and start leading your big life, your way!

### *STEP 1*

You may have heard of the goal-setting acronym SMART before. It suggests all goals should be:

- Specific
- Measurable
- Achievable

- Realistic
- Timebound

So, for your goal make it specific, identify how you'll measure your success, check it's achievable and realistic (although it's likely to be stretching for you from where you are now), and set a timescale for when you want to achieve it by.

For example:

- If you want to feel more confident, how much more confident and by when? What will have to happen for you to know that you've achieved this level of confidence?
- Maybe you want to learn a new language - what level do you want to achieve by when? How will you know you have achieved it?
- Is your goal to get fit? How fit? Do you want to be able to run a marathon, run 10k in under 60 minutes, be able to walk for 30 minutes continuously or be able to touch your toes? When do you want to achieve this? Based on your current fitness levels is the goal achievable in the timeframe you have set out?
- Do you want to get a promotion? What job/grade do you want? By when? Based on your current level of

experience and the timescale you want, is this a
realistic and achievable goal?

If something isn't achievable or realistic at this stage, that's
okay! It just means it may take longer to achieve and/or you
may want to set some smaller goals to get you from where
you are now to your end goal. This is useful information and
will help you when you create your plan!

### STEP 2

Spend some time understanding your 'why': Why is this goal
important to you? Why do you want to achieve it?

We have talked about this earlier in the book, but it is really
important because when things get tough (and things do get
tough), you will need to have that inner motivation to keep
going because you have a real desire for the end result.

Ask yourself: Why is this goal important to me? Now ask
yourself: So what? Write down your answer in your journal,
and then ask yourself again: So what? Repeat this five or
more times.

This helps you dig past your conscious thoughts of why you
think something is important to you and starts to delve into
your unconscious reasons for wanting to achieve this.

Now answer these questions:

- What will achieving this goal give you?
- How will achieving your goal look, sound and feel to you?
- On a scale of 1 to 10 (with 1 being not at all committed and 10 being totally committed), how committed are you to achieving your goal?
- If the response is below a 10, what needs to happen for you to be totally committed to achieving your goal?

You now have a very specific goal with a clear understanding of why this is important for you to achieve it.

## STEP 3

Let's now focus on what could stop you from achieving this goal.

So the first question for you: Why have you not achieved this goal previously?

It is time to get brutally honest with yourself because it's only then can you face these obstacles and overcome them. It might be that:

- you didn't find the time
- you fear what other people think of you
- it wasn't as important as other things
- you didn't have the money

- you find it nicer to stay in bed for an extra hour than to get up when it was cold outside
- you have a friend you can't say no to
- you spend hours scrolling through your social media accounts
- you preferred to binge-watch the latest series on Netflix

There is no judgement in any of this. It isn't that you have 'failed' previously, you're just collecting feedback.

You can then use this information to help answer the next question: What is going to be different this time?

Maybe you need to spend 15 minutes journaling a day to keep reminding yourself of what you're grateful for, or what you have achieved in a day. Maybe you need to start training in summer, so it's a habit by the colder winter months to go for daily runs. Maybe you need to get your clothes ready the night before so you can have 10 minutes for your meditation practice in the morning. Maybe you need to limit your social media browsing to 30 minutes in the evening to free up your time to learn a new language or complete the online course you want to finish.

Thinking about and having strategies to overcome or remove obstacles is going to help give you the very best chance of success.

## STEP 4

Having created a SMART goal, you know your timescale for achieving this, which may be short or long. Either way, there will be actions that you need to take - so now you need to identify exactly what steps are required for you to achieve your goal.

You'll need to work out if you prefer working from where you are to your goal, or envisaging the goal and working backwards.

An example of moving from where you are now to where you want to be could be if you have a goal to increase your friendship circle or professional network by the end of the year. You may decide your first step is to join some online forums and groups on Facebook and LinkedIn. After a few weeks of online activity, you may decide to then attend a local networking event, or a class, to meet people in person. Once you have connected with some like-minded people in your local community, you may decide to ask one or two of them if they want to meet for a coffee, etc.

If you prefer to work backwards from the end goal and if you're looking for a promotion by the end of the year, for example: it might be that you know by November you'll need to have an updated CV, by October you'll need to have achieved X training/qualification, by June you'll need to have had a development conversation with your manager, etc.

There isn't a right or wrong way of doing any of this; it's about finding what works for you, and creating a plan and then executing against this so you can see the progress you're making towards achieving your end goal.

## STEP 5

So you now have a well-defined goal set for yourself, you know why it's important to you, you have removed the obstacles to achieving it (or have an awareness of them and thought of strategies to overcome them), and you have a step-by-step action plan.

You now need to focus on motivation and how you keep taking consistent actions to move you forward. For you, this may be the obstacle you identified in step 3, but for many of us, we find starting out on a goal is easy, but it's when that initial 'buzz' has worn off, and the hard work and the reality of the situation sets in, that we then find our motivation dips.

So here are a couple of ideas to consider:

1. Refer back to your why - remind yourself of the reasons you're doing this, what it will give you, why it's important to you, what success looks, feels and sounds like for you. Anchor these feelings and know that any short-term discomfort you're feeling will be outweighed by the immense feelings of

accomplishment on following through and achieving your goal.

2. Ask yourself what the one action you can commit to do today to move you towards your goal is? And this action can be as small as you like - it's just about maintaining progress. By doing this, you're taking your focus from something big and daunting to something small and very achievable. You will get a sense of achievement when you accomplish this. Momentum breeds momentum. Do this every day, and you'll be amazed at the progress you make.

And if you're really still struggling, ask yourself, is this actually that important to me? Review your initial 'why' - has anything changed? This isn't about flaking on your goals or not following through, but it's about being honest and kind to yourself. Life sometimes takes over, other priorities come up, and you have to put something on the back burner. It may be that the timing is now wrong or you need to re-evaluate the timeline. Or maybe, as you're working towards something, you're uncovering information that makes you realise that what you thought you wanted isn't actually what you want. This is okay. Go back through this exercise and set yourself a new goal, taking all that you have learnt from your experience to be able to define and set a new meaningful goal to work towards, that's right for you now.

## WHAT NOW?

This book has shared with you lots of ideas, insights, and exercises for you to work through so you can create a life you love, and show up as the bright, brave, bold, brilliant woman I know you are, and hopefully, you're believing this about yourself too!

I suggest giving yourself time to really explore these activities. Self-development is continuous work and can be difficult at times. Be kind to yourself.

Having tried all the exercises, select the techniques that resonate with you the most and keep doing them. Concentrate on 1-2 ideas to implement fully, and once you have embedded these in your life, you can try some other ones to keep building your confidence and finding ways to reduce self-doubt. Also, I suggest trying the ones that didn't work last time [again] to see if you get a different result next time. Be an experimenter in your own life and always be curious. The more you do this, the more self-awareness you'll gain. You have so many tools now to build your confidence, so start using them!

Remember, if you can change or improve by 1% a day, in just over three months you will have changed or improved by 100% from where you are now!

## Coaching

I accept that no-one needs a coach, and probably one of the reasons you invested in this book is because you know how effective you are at learning new things and making changes. With the right motivation and mindset, you can definitely achieve all of your goals and behavioural changes by yourself. The answers are all within you already, and it's up to you to take the actions.

However, there are times you may need a little extra help. A coach can help you achieve your results faster, more efficiently and often exceed your own expectations.

I have coached individuals to:

- deepen their self-awareness so they can understand themselves better and make choices that are more aligned to living a life that is authentic to them
- achieve their business goals by removing mindset issues around money
- understand what confidence means to them and how to increase this so they could go for a promotion at work

- reduce anxiety so they can sleep on a Sunday evening, ahead of work on a Monday
- have strategies that work for them to overcome feelings of being an imposter
- create and action a plan to achieve a particular study goal in a set timeframe
- design and execute on a professional development plan to secure a job promotion
- cultivate a more positive mindset as they were fed up with always seeing the downside of situations

A coach can support you, be your cheerleader, be your confidant, have total belief in you, and hold your goal as your anchor to help guide your decisions and actions. They can help you gain new perspectives and uncover those elusive blind spots that may be holding you back!

Athletes and sports professionals know the benefits of continuous coaching. It would seem ludicrous if an Olympian achieves gold and then sacks their coach because they are top of their game and no longer needs them. Instead, they continue to want to improve, beat their own personal best, to keep getting better and to always be the best they can be.

If you're needing some additional help in achieving your goals, here are some of the key reasons investing in a coach works:

## ACCOUNTABILITY

When I asked a client why they enjoy coaching so much, they explained it was because they are an entrepreneur and our coaching sessions do two things for her: it holds her accountable to her business progress and growth, and gives her another professional to discuss things with.

I know the accountability part is the main reason coaching is so effective for me. I don't want to turn up to the next session, not having completed what I had committed to do. Even when I try to play out a really good excuse in my head, I know it sounds weak, especially against the commitment I had to the task in the last session. So, I start to make progress and hold myself accountable for both the results I do, and don't, achieve - because there are times life gets in the way, or something is actually far more difficult or time-consuming than you originally planned for! There are teachings in all situations and working with your own coach helps you to take these, learn and grow from them.

Other clients I work with agree with this, stating they know they can achieve things by themselves, but change is hard. Having to check in with someone on a regular basis keeps you focused. Action is the way to implement change and to move forward. A literal definition of a coach is the vehicle to take you from one place to another. It is a journey; it's about moving from where you are to where you want to be. It's not to say that we occasionally don't take a wrong path or a more scenic route than was originally imagined, but it is always forward-moving and heading in the [general!] right direction.

## MOTIVATION

Keeping motivated, even if you're clear on your purpose, can sometimes still be difficult. Change can be uncomfortable. It is about doing something new and challenging, and it is about being consistent, and I know, personally, I needed to be supported to 'step up' within my own career and business. You may seek coaching to break down the actions required to achieve an outcome, but I find both with clients, and from my own personal experience, it can also be about internal changes in your thinking and mindset.

Understanding your own limiting beliefs - often things you're totally unaware of until someone asks that question that shines a spotlight on your blind spot - and the ways you think about something which may not be the most helpful to you, can be hugely liberating when you get that 'break-through' and what has been [invisibly] holding you back for years has gone. It's valuable when you get a different perspective, or someone gently but firmly holds up that mirror and asks those sometimes challenging questions that mean you change how you view a situation or yourself and can find the determination to keep going.

## RETURN ON INVESTMENT

Investing in a coach is just that - an investment. It's an investment of your money, but it's also an investment of your time, an investment of your energy and an investment in yourself. It is about achieving something you have always wanted to achieve or developing a skill you have always wanted to develop, or it's about deepening your self-awareness to feel truly confident, or removing that limiting belief so you can excel in your career and life. It's giving yourself permission to explore, to dream, to take action and to make changes that will move you from where you are now to where you want to be. It's having someone who totally believes in you and your potential, someone who will hold the space for you, as well as being your accountability partner to ensure you remain on track to achieve your goals.

It's your journey, you're responsible for the outcomes, and you do have all the answers within you, but a coach can help unlock this potential, hold you up, and take some of the weight when the uphill paths feel a bit steep. A great coach can keep you moving to that summit, reminding you of the views you so desperately want to see at the top and breaking down the journey into manageable steps so you can get there. Compare this to the alternative - you stop and head back down to where you came from as you find it's just too hard to keep going on your own.

If you're ready to achieve your goals, deepen your self-awareness and/or make your desired behavioural changes, and you want professional help, please feel free to have a nose around my website - www.lindseyhood.net - to see if I might be the coach for you!

## LETS BE SOCIAL

It has been an absolute privilege to support you in over-coming imposter syndrome, quieting your self-doubt, and building your confidence.

I would love to hear about your success stories and the exercises that particularly worked for you, as your stories can also help and inspire others. You can contact and connect with me on:

**Facebook:** facebook.com/lindseyhoodlifecoach
**Instagram:** instagram.com/lindseyhoodlifecoach
**LinkedIn:** www.linkedin.com/in/lindseyhood
**Email:** lindsey@lindseyhood.net

Remember, I believe in you, and you now have the strategies to re-believe in yourself so you can create and lead your own big life, in a quiet way!

Thank you and good luck!

## TESTIMONIALS

I'm passionate about what I do and love coaching and empowering women. Here is a small selection of testimonials from some of the amazing women I've helped.

---

"Lindsey has worked with me during several times in my life where I needed guidance and help in working out my options and creating a clear plan of action. I find Lindsey to be very patient and has a warm, caring energy. She is very encouraging and positive. Working with her really helped me work out what I wanted to achieve and what I needed to do to get there. I would definitely recommend her to other people who are looking to enhance their lives and build on their successes."

— CLAIRE IBBOTSON

---

"Lindsey excels in motivating and coaching individuals, her positive outlook and hard work is a credit to her own success. The support she has given me with my own development plan and building my inner confidence has enabled me to be able to take the next steps in achieving my future aspirations. Thank you."

— SUZANNE WELLS

"I used to become very anxious about things I couldn't control, which began to affect my professional and personal life. Lindsey kindly agreed to work with me to address this, and I can honestly say, this was the best decision I have ever made! Even though I have met Lindsey briefly in a social environment, she was nothing but professional during our session and made me feel at ease about sharing such a personal issue. She gave me some really valuable exercises I could do if I began to feel anxious, and I have continued to use these in day to day life. If you are looking for a life coach, I would say your search is now over as you have found the best around!"

— NADINE WEST

"I really enjoyed the coaching sessions and feel more focused on what I need to do going forward. Thank you for your time and your non-judgment of my thoughts and feelings. It's always daunting opening up but thank you for creating a safe space for me to do that."

— NISHA HAQ

"Lindsey has been supporting me to identify and secure promotion at work. She has helped me prioritise and focus on my strengths in order to give me more confidence and motivation. Lindsey has challenged me to think with a different perspective which has helped me to broaden my outlook and seek new challenges to support my ongoing development. Thank you so much for your help and support Lindsey xx"

— CARLA JEFFERSON

"Lindsey is an amazing coach. Kind, understanding and full of great ideas. I am so glad I found her. It was a year ago we started our coaching sessions. I was lacking in direction as to how to push my business forward and get the balance right in my personal life. Lindsey helped me to work through which way to progress, guided me to set goals (for which she held me accountable) and helped me to review business progress and keep moving forward.

One year on, I can happily say my business and I are thriving. Lindsey's coaching had such an impact on my business confidence and the way I view myself in my industry. The result of this has been a significant uplift in terms of the quality of clients I am attracting, and as a result, my income has almost tripled. Thank you, Lindsey, you're the best!"

— SUSIE HARRIS

"Lindsey is an absolute superstar! Loved every minute of our session and, as always, I've come away invigorated! Thank you for helping me remember me!"

— NADIA REFAE

"Lindsey helped me through coaching just after I had taken voluntary redundancy last year. I wanted to take time to open my mind and explore the possible choices that might be available, rather than just continue to do what was familiar. She was excellent at asking just the right questions to draw out thoughts and facilitate my answers. Lindsey has a perfect approach, never pushing, just allowing and prompting at the right moments. She capably steered me over bumpy periods when the straight path became a little challenging and inspired me to think positively about what is important to me. I highly recommend Lindsey as the person to guide you through times of change and growth in a supportive, empowering way. Thank you!"

— Sara Greenwood

# REFERENCES

## Chapter 2 - Imposter Syndrome

1. The Imposter Phenomenon in High Achieving Women: Dynamics and Therapeutic Intervention - Pauline Rose Clance & Suzanne Imes - Published in Psychotherapy Theory, Research and Practice Volume 15, #3, Fall 1978
2. The Imposter Phenomenon in High Achieving Women: Dynamics and Therapeutic Intervention - Pauline Rose Clance & Suzanne Imes - Published in Psychotherapy Theory, Research and Practice Volume 15, #3, Fall 1978
3. The Imposter Phenomenon: Recent Research Findings Regarding Dynamics, Personality and Family Patterns and Their Implications for Treatment - Joe Langford & Pauline Clance - Published by Psychotherapy, Volume 30, #3, Fall 1993
4. Presence: Bringing Your Boldest Self to Your Biggest Challenges - Amy Cuddy - Published by Orion Publishing Co, 2016
5. Power Your Presence - Research from International Center for Research on Women and TRESemmé, 2019: https://www.tresemme.com/uk/poweryourpresence.html
6. The Imposter Phenomenon in High Achieving Women: Dynamics and Therapeutic Intervention - Pauline Rose Clance & Suzanne Imes - Published in Psychotherapy Theory, Research and Practice Volume 15, #3, Fall 1978
7. The Secret Thoughts of Successful Women: Why Capable People Suffer from the Impostor Syndrome and How to Thrive in Spite of It - Valerie Young, Ed.D. - Published by Crown Business, 2011
8. The Secret Thoughts of Successful Women: Why Capable People Suffer from the Impostor Syndrome and How to Thrive in Spite of It - Valerie Young, Ed.D. - Published by Crown Business, 2011
9. The Imposter Phenomenon: Overcoming The Fear That Haunts Your

Success - Dr. Pauline Rose Clance - Published by Peachtree Publishers, Ltd., 1985

10. What Is Confidence and Why Is It Important? - Lindsey Hood - White Paper published in 2018

11. Michelle Obama: I still have imposter syndrome - Reported on BBC News, 4th December 2018: www.bbc.co.uk/news/uk-46434147

12. Power Your Presence - Research from International Center for Research on Women and TRESemmé, 2019: https://www.tresemme.com/uk/poweryourpresence.html

13. The Art of Extraordinary Confidence: Your Ultimate Path to Love, Wealth, and Freedom - Dr. Aziz Gazipura - Published by B.C. Allen Publishing, 2016

14. In The Company of Women: Inspiration and Advice from over 100 Makers, Artists, and Entrepreneurs - Grace Bonney - Published by Artisan, 2016

15. Celebrities struggling with imposter syndrome - Google search conducted on 17th November 2019: www.google.com

16. Princess Beatrice reveals she looks for ways to 'be authentic' as she opens up about having 'impostor syndrome' - reported on Mail Online, 6th December 2019: https://www.dailymail.co.uk/femail/article-7763635/Princess-Beatrice-reveals-suffers-Imposter-Syndrome-day.html

# Chapter 3 - Self-Awareness

1. Self Awareness - Pathway to Happiness blog post - first written 11th May 2015; updated 18th September 2019. Accessed on 24th November 2019: https://pathwaytohappiness.com/blog/self-awareness/

2. The power of believing you can improve - Carol Dweck - TedX Norrkoping, November 2014: https://www.ted.com/talks/carol_dweck_the_power_of_believing_that_you_can_improve?utm_campaign=tedspread&utm_medium=referral&utm_source=tedcomshare

3. Do Less, Get More: Guilt-free Ways to Make time for the Things (and People) that Matter - Sháá Wasmund - Published by Penguin Life, 2016

# Chapter 4 - Values and Motivation

1. Collins English Dictionary - Accessed online in 2019: https://www.collinsdictionary.com/
2. The Secret Thoughts of Successful Women: Why Capable People Suffer from the Impostor Syndrome and How to Thrive in Spite of It - Valerie Young, Ed.D. - Published by Crown Business, 2011
3. Collins English Dictionary - Accessed online in 2019: https://www.collinsdictionary.com/
4. Motivational Mapping: A unique approach to coaching - Bevis Moynan - Webinar for the Association for Coaching - 12th November 2019
5. The Power of Leverage: Creating lasting change skill session - Anthony Robbins -https://www.tonyrobbins.com/resources/pdfs/The-Power-of-Leverage.pdf

# Chapter 5 - Confidence

1. Collins English Dictionary - Accessed online in 2019: https://www.collinsdictionary.com/
2. What Is Confidence and Why Is It Important? - Lindsey Hood - White Paper published in 2018
3. Feel The Fear And Do It Anyway: How to Turn Your Fear and Indecision into Confidence and Action - Susan Jeffers - Published by Vermilion, 2007 (revised edition)
4. The Confidence Code: The Science and Art of Self-Assurance - What Women Should Know - Katty Kay & Claire Shipman - Published by Harper Business, 2014
5. Caroline Miller, quoted in The Confidence Code: The Science and Art of Self-Assurance - What Women Should Know - Katty Kay & Claire Shipman - Published by Harper Business, 2014
6. How Much Data is Created on the Internet Each Day? - Micro Focus blog post by Jeff Schultz, Published 8th June 2019. Accessed 9th December 2019: https://blog.microfocus.com/how-much-data-is-created-on-the-internet-each-day/

7. The Imposter Phenomenon in High Achieving Women: Dynamics and Therapeutic Intervention - Pauline Rose Clance & Suzanne Imes - Published in Psychotherapy Theory, Research and Practice Volume 15, #3, Fall 1978

8. Your body language may shape who you are - Amy Cuddy - TedGlobal 2012                                    https://www.ted.com/talks/ amy_cuddy_your_body_language_may_shape_who_you_are? utm_campaign=tedspread&utm_medium=referral& utm_source=tedcomshare

9. How to Create Unstoppable Success - Marie Forleo - Live event at Central Hall, Westminster, London on 9th October 2019

## Chapter 6 - Tuning Into Your Inner Voice

1. The Imposter Cure: How to stop feeling like a fraud and escape the mind-trap of imposter syndrome - Dr Jessamy Hibberd - Published by Aster, 2019

## Chapter 7 - How To Believe In Yourself Again

1. The War of Art: Break Through the Blocks and Win Your Inner Creative Battles - Steve Pressfield - Published by Black Irish Entertainment LLC, 2012

2. You Are a Badass: How to Stop Doubting Your Greatness and Start Living an Awesome Life - Jen Sincero - Published by John Murray Learning, 2016

3. Making Habits, Breaking Habits: Why We Do Things, Why We Don't, and How to Make Any Change Stick - Jeremy Dean - Published by Oneworld Publications, 2013

# Chapter 8 - Aligning Your Inner and Outer Worlds

1. Choose Wonder Over Worry: Move Beyond Fear and Doubt to Unlock your Full Potential - Amber Rae - Published by Piatkus, 2018
2. How to Kill Imposter Syndrome and Speak with Confidence - Minnie von Mallinckrodt-Grant - Webinar for the Institute of Leadership & Management (ILM) - 18th December 2019

# Chapter 10 - Starting To Lead Your Big Life

1. Failure is part of success - Eduardo Zanatta - TEDxBYU, April 2012 https://youtu.be/bujIb_sQZvQ

Printed in Great Britain
by Amazon

47344120R00119